NORTH OF DARKNESS

Elaine Poulin

NORTH OF DARKNESS

A Classic Perceptions Publication

Translation by: Bernard A. Poulin

Cover design by: Bernard A. Poulin

Proofreading by: Heather Lee Parker

Graphic design by: Emilie Drolet-Gratton

Copyright © 2017 CLASSIC PERCEPTIONS

perceptionsclassiques@outlook.com

ISBN: 978-2-9814225-4-5

All rights reserved. No part of this book may be reproduced, stored or transmitted by any means—whether auditory, graphic, mechanical or electronic—without written consent of the publisher except in the use of brief excerpts used in critical articles and reviews. Unauthorized reproduction of any part of this work is illegal and is punishable by law.

The author and the publisher disclaim all liability as to the use of the information contained in this book. The contents are provided as information only.

Printed in the USA by Lulu Publishing
www.lulu.com

Dedication

To my beloved Michael, for his undaunted strength, his openness, his patience, his love.

Contents

Foreword 9

Introduction 11

Chapter 1: Leaving for Africa 13

Chapter 2: In the Heart of Burkina Faso 17

Chapter 3: Returning Home 47

Chapter 4: The Diagnosis 53

Chapter 5: The Road to Recovery 59

Chapter 6: Rebuilding my Life 99

Chapter 7: A Support Network 109

Chapter 8: The Future: Being Free, Reborn 117

Chapter 9: Beyond Post-Traumatic Stress Disorder 121

Annex 1 143

References 161

Acknowledgements 163

Chapter 2 "In the Heart of Burkina Faso" discusses traumatic content. It may trigger PTSD symptoms. If you are feeling triggered, skip ahead to Chapter 9. There, I share ideas for dealing with stress and provide a "Toolbox" that may help both you and those who support you.

With best wishes,

Elaine Poulin

Foreword

With sensitive and truly moving dialogue, Elaine Poulin gives us the opportunity to walk in the footsteps of another's life lived, to take part in her long and painful struggle to regain footing after a devastating diagnosis of post-traumatic stress disorder and depression. On her 10-month journey in Africa, we encounter the diametrically opposed complexities of a country called Burkina Faso where *"the richness of individuals and their culture clashes incessantly with the relentless weight of everyday life."*

In the end, Elaine cannot adjust to or cope with the constant upheavals that constitute the daily existence in which she finds herself. Unable to adapt to her new surroundings, an ever widening fissure begins to scar her soul. With the gradual loss of her bearings, she eventually loses her way. Without a compass, she can no longer recognize, nor take in, the particulars that nebulously define her place within this unknown world she has entered. She feels excluded, isolated. With time, she is no longer able to reconcile her needs with those of her adopted environment.

Elaine Poulin demystifies post-traumatic stress disorder. In this book, she opens her heart to scrutiny. She lays bare the psychological injuries and the scarring that eat away at those who suffer at the hands of serious traumas. Along with confronting the feelings of impotence encountered, she gives credence to the devastating experiences lived, and invites any and all of those who suffer likewise to come out of the shadows, to live life as fully as is possible, despite this illness called post-traumatic stress disorder.

North of Darkness adds much to our understanding of suffering; to the understanding of the deep sense of abandonment felt and re-felt by first-responders, soldiers and police—those who, over and above encountering devastating situations in the service of their communities, must face the greatest of enemies: powerlessness in the face of a psychological black depth, which little by little engulfs us whole. We are all thankful to Elaine for having demystified, rendered real, the nature of this wound.

LGen, the Honourable Roméo Dallaire, Senator (ret.)

Introduction

When a heartbeat skips . . . disrupting essential life rhythms . . . When life takes a spin into chaos. When anxiety invades every moment of every day. When everything begins to crumble, when a once gregarious soul shatters . . . It is difficult to define the crippling goings-on from within; the devastating crashes from without. What then?

Between the dream and the reality of taking on a task of international humanitarian aid, between the departure from homeland and my transition back to Canada—that return to a "me" state—there were, there are, my writings. In them, my story. I wanted to look back upon my adventure but through the use of a new prism, a perspective other than one tainted by an initial desire to help, by a renewal of justice and generosity throughout the world. In essence, the goal became one of sharing a new motive; one of reflections on reality, with the question being: Should I have gone off on this adventure? Should I have not?

That being said, this book goes beyond telling a story that is strictly mine. For, when illness comes calling . . . how do we continue living despite the pressures of newly acquired limits? What does it take to transform suffering, to thrive rather than simply to survive?

And so, on the road to recovery, I held fast to those writings. In the form of a book, they anchored me. They rendered credible the experiences and sufferings I had encountered. In essence, the negatives were transformed, opening a door to freedom—as partial as that was.

The major portion of *North of Darkness* was written in spare moments, in "fits of possibility." Interspersed, one paragraph at a time, here and there within the confinement of my illness, I wrote. All in all, this book has become the tool through which I have been able to heal my wounds.

I can only wish that it offers hope to those who suffer from mental illness and/or gives comfort to those affected by post-traumatic stress disorder. I pray that it helps break the binds of solitude afflicting soldiers, journalists, police officers, firemen, emergency personnel, humanitarian aid volunteers and professionals, and all those who live with a debilitating illness for whatever reason—and who suffer in silence—in the shadows of desperation.

Thank you for reading . . .

Affectionately,

Elaine

Chapter 1: Leaving for Africa

It is 2003. I am at a turning point in my life. For the past seven years I've successfully run my own gourmet food business. Nonetheless, I feel empty. I spend several months wondering . . . why, what for, where to next? I want to make a difference in the lives of others—a difference that goes beyond delicious apricot jams and Grand Marnier jellies, beyond smiling at customers and tempting palates with the sensual nature of sinful sweets. I'm looking for something deeper, but I don't know what.

In my prayers, I ask my guardian angel for guidance. One splendid spring evening, the answer comes to me in the shape of a dream. In that dream, I am in a room filled with seriously ill patients. Someone calls out to me, asks me to feed a man in his early forties, a man dying of cancer. He is shy and reticent. I take his frailty into my arms, and present him with my breast. As he drinks, I caress his hair. When I awake, I am overcome with an indescribable peace. My new vocation unfolds before me. The doubts and questions and wonderings fade away. A decision is made . . . We, my husband and I, will go off to tend to those in need.

Goodbye paradise . . .

October 2005

We sell our house, our 75-acre paradise, our ancient yet charming country retreat with its 1200-square-foot barn transformed by hand into a creativity and production centre for my small enterprise. During the hot summer months, its cool interior often welcomed us.

The decision to sell the fruit of seven years' hard labor was difficult for me. But then, managing renters from a distance is not appealing. And still . . . there is a nagging fear . . . I cringe at going off on a quest and eventually coming back home—but to nothing; to no anchoring space.

And so, several couple discussions later, several compromises considered, decisions are taken and we move on . . . Africa bids us to come. Leaving the known is difficult. But the adventure, the gift of giving calls.

I love travelling and all of its inherent cultural considerations. Discovering is always wondrous. For many years now, I have dreamed of completing my trip around the world—a trip started so many years ago. Africa was the last continent to be added to my agenda. From Costa Rica to Thailand, from Australia to Italy, from New Zealand to Fiji, each voyage urged me on to the next discovery. My backpack is well seasoned. But despite this wanderlust, it was in Vietnam that I yearned to finally settle down. But now, Africa smiles, and so my adventurous spirit and newfound missionary zeal conquer all hesitations.

The months before our departure are filled with signs . . . Africa is everywhere—in the streets, on the radio, in my dreams. The goal is to discover both the human and the spiritual within me and within the parameters of the quest itself. I want, I need to connect . . . to become one with those in need. I want to live with them, to accompany them, to encourage those who suffer that there is more for them than just suffering. In my deepest thoughts, I want to be an instrument of peace, of hope and of justice.

But how to prepare? In 2005, before our departure, I choose to work as a volunteer among the street people, those who are ill. And it is they who confirm that my decision, my new direction, is a good one. And yet . . . a small dark cloud floats high above; too near to be ignored, too far to be understood . . . A nagging question rises. Is it necessary to go to the ends of the earth to help our neighbours, to make a difference in the disenfranchised lives of the many in need?

The day of the first departure arrives. I stand alone before my roots, my little house on the prairie. I caress the cat. She too is to be left behind. For the first time since we acquired our house, I am sad . . . saddened by the Monet beauty of it all on this pristine fall day. I sense danger . . . a weakness in the knees, an indescribable fright overtakes me. Amid an assortment of suitcases piled one atop another I sit in the car, numbed, crushed by our decision. I suddenly cry a profound desperate cry . . .

I cry for the once bright dream of aging contentedly with my spouse in this idyllic, this magic setting. The very idea that it is too late burns a hole in me. That I cannot go back is the deepest cut. But I must leave . . . The sale of the property is confirmed. I had anticipated a feeling of liberation, of joy at the audacity of our plans. What a surprise to find my feelings to be at the extreme opposite of my goals.

Inserting the key into the ignition is difficult. The ever-curving road between Ripon and Thurso is near-impossible to see through this torrent of tears.

We chose to throw caution to the winds, to place our fate in the hands of life's unknowns. We freed ourselves from material possessions as a proactive measure of our commitment—as a precursor to signing a contract that would commit us to Africa. And so, furniture and precious personal memorabilia are stored. Renting a small furnished apartment, we live out of our suitcases. For the next two months we wait . . . The sudden exaltation of being free, unattached, without responsibilities hits . . . And yet, in equal and opposite measure, and with eerie intensity, apprehensions rise as the challenge becomes more and more the unknown, and less and less the anticipated adventure. In essence, we are embarking upon an unknown ship to an unknown place with unknown qualities and challenges—and all experienced in an atmosphere of being nowhere, being attached to nothing and knowing even less of what awaits . . . That was our place in the grand scheme of our own making.

It is not until two months later that my husband signs a contract with an NGO. Following an interview to corroborate his credentials, previous experience, educational qualifications and professional competencies related to the contracted position, we are offered a 15-

hour introductory course to international work. As a spouse, it is highly recommended that I also attend these sessions, this sole obligatory series of sessions related to this organization. In those five modules, 15 hours, the subject matter goes from cooperation to development, from past efforts to contemporary methodologies. We are given an overview of humanitarian aid and reconstruction, globalization and socio-economic structures in light of poverty elimination strategies, political environments as they relate to development, cooperation and cultural parameters.

With courses completed, I stow away in one of our suitcases my accreditation and study documents—as if they are passports to this new world we have been invited to enter. And so, we leave for Burkina Faso in January of 2006 for our ten-month stint.

Chapter 2: In the Heart of Burkina Faso

The shock . . .

January 2006

A tiny hand reaches for mine. A large smile stretching from ear to ear on his wondrously beautiful face, he presents to me his noon-day meal; possibly the only one he will enjoy that day. Approximately 10, he pads along beside me; barefoot. His graceful presence lights the path leading to my house. Every day, each noon, he greets me. As I pedal my bike towards him, he offers to me, shares with me his food. His candour, his generosity, both are balms to his entreaty: "Nassara, you are invited!"

Cycling back from the marketplace, I notice him in the lane, engrossed in a world of games. His toys? Two metal cans joined by a string. Like the others, he plays enthusiastically throughout the area, avoiding pig feces and potholes.

On one side of the street, flowering shrubs enliven the rich exterior of a cement-walled villa. On the opposite side, a stark mud village house. Burkina Faso is a land of immense contrasts.

Finally home, I lie exhausted—stretched across my mattress on the earthen floor, crushed by the heat to which I know I must become accustomed. Lizards skitter up and down the walls ignoring the thousands of miniature ants marching hurriedly, obediently, efficiently along a path that has been laid out for them—a path stretching from one wall of my personal space to the other.

Later, in my room, alone, I sit on a bamboo chair . . . Outside there is an incessant buzz. Life here is lived noisily, intensely—and this from morning 'til night. I struggle to create an interior oasis, a respite within myself—a calm place where I can more easily absorb this oh so different life, this so differently configured and so never-endingly animated life.

Images of my arrival scroll past... From Koudougou to Ouagadougou... a 2-hour bus ride... you come to us, to welcome us, to accompany us to our new home... It's hot, very hot. Sweat darkens your skin—my pale whiteness a startling contrast to yours. We shake hands. Miraculously, all the tiredness fades; your greeting defined by a huge smile offered up to 2 exhausted strangers. You take us to an outdoor restaurant where others with whom we will be working add even more to the warmth already proffered. Without a doubt, we are made to feel completely welcome in this, your land. The imprint of your hand remains in mine—a symbol of your humanity, your people. It is you who are rich. It is me who is poor.

During the long road to Koudougou I look for a store to buy a snack. There are none. Just a series of old tables or canvas sheets laid out on the side of the road. Everywhere there is garbage and in the air horrible smells to which I must become accustomed. There are no sidewalks. There are no gutters or sewer systems. In essence, there is no infrastructure whatsoever. Roads are nothing more than irregularly surfaced directional indicators upon which bicycles, motorcycles, pedestrians, dogs, goats, pigs and pull carts mix with a few more-insistent cars. Arid dust is everywhere, rendered heavy by the smells of ill-burned diesel fuel, human and animal excrement and garbage. Combined, the colourless specter rises heavily with the passing of each body and vehicle.

Despite wanting to take in this new adventure with an open heart, I feel nauseous... The shock to the system is immense. In between reluctant breaths, I am enveloped by a sudden darkness.

First night: Though I try to make out the parameters of this tiny village—of which I will be a part for the next 10 months of my life—I can't. The darkness of the night is thicker than the dust in the air. I can't see you... I can only recognize the smell of your skin.

Life in the village

My eyes are closed, hair foamed with soap. Something wriggles over my foot. I look down. A cockroach... I scream! Florence[1] comes running and laughs uproariously.

Despite the lack of hot water, I try to finish washing my hair. Shit! Now, the water is cut off... again. Luckily I have a full pail with which I can rinse my hair. Nonetheless, I have to remember to ration for the household, for showers, for cooking. Maybe I could have someone negotiate for a reservoir with the proprietor of the house. Doing it myself would be impossible.

On African soil, the family and hierarchy are everything. The clan plays a major role in the unfolding of society. Family is the cement of African culture. It is unusually large by North American standards: its membership being the husband, the wife (or wives), the children, the cousins. One of the most fundamental values in the family structure here is mutual support. Everyone spends a lot of time with each other. Families, therefore, live near or with one another. And at the head of every family is a man.

A clan is made up of all those who have one ancestor or another in common. At the head of each clan is the Council of Elders—and once again, they are all men.

I must quickly get used to the idea that women are not seen to be equal here. Cultural differences in this regard will undoubtedly make my relationships with male colleagues difficult. But I am not intimidated. It actually reinforces my resolve and the compassion I feel for Florence who, after leaving an abusive husband, is raising her son alone—and this despite the objections of her society and family who would much prefer she had submitted and endured. I am moved by Florence's enthusiasm; her lust for life, her capacity to remain positive in difficult situations. A typical portrait of Burkina Faso women, she is proud, strong, resilient, hard-working, generous, and spontaneously joyous and giggly. I often hear Florence's laughter filling the air the moment she encounters a family member. With one

---

[1] Housekeeper/ Roumarou's mother

of the local guards, she finds great pleasure in teasing and poking. Often, she arrives for work sporting a new hairdo, a cellular phone to her ear, always meticulously attired and clean. Proud of her work as a domestic with the "whites," this standing gives her a certain status within the Burkina Faso community.

I become very appreciative of having a housekeeper—someone to clean, wash, cook meals and run errands—as I discover the scope of each task. Much as there are many advantages to having "help," there is also an immediate sense that intimacy has been lost. As modesty is an integral part of the Burkina Faso culture, my husband and I begin to touch less, display physical affection less, both in public and at home.

My first challenge, therefore, is adaptation. Everything needs it. The country, the people, the culture, the heat, the living conditions, the extreme poverty. Surprisingly, it is to the dust and extreme heat (35 to 45 degrees Celsius) to which I first become accustomed.

I came to Africa expecting and hoping to live as simply as possible. I do not want "distances" between me, "the white woman," and you, Burkinabé. I want to live as you do in your country. I want to work and commune with you, my brothers, my sisters . . . But it is difficult. Whether I wish it or not, the colour of my skin is a barrier. It taints our relationship, with you who in 1960 declared independence for your people. And next to the so many always hungry and illiterate, it is impossible to not be different since I am not a part of your history, your story.

I decide to take on the organization of our living spaces. At first, the idea seems simple enough, but a second glance soon reveals many subtle complexities involved in that plan. Ousmane, an acquaintance, graciously offers to accompany me, to negotiate the construction of a base for our bed. Sleeping atop a foam mattress on the earthen floor has become difficult. My back aches horribly. My growing impatience is a direct result of this discomfort.

Two weeks later, I head off to Koudougou. I have no clue why my bed base has not yet been delivered. Astride my pink bicycle, I negotiate the rough dust-filled roads leading to the main street. Pedaling is difficult. The city heat, suffocating.

Once I arrive at the door of the carpenter shop, a solution to my dilemma is not at hand... I must first find someone who speaks French. Only a very small portion of the population is educated, and only those who are speak French. Despite language school and my numerous efforts to learn the *Moré* dialect, I remain incapable of translating or communicating my thoughts to the *Burkinabés*.

With a newly found translator in tow, I ask why my bed is not ready. Ousmane had been emphatic, his negotiations conclusive. What is the problem? It is simple. The carpenter wants more money. I stare at him in disbelief. He stares back smiling. I am caught in a trap. To emphasize his demand, he explains that nothing has been started on my project. I finally submit, handing over the equivalent of $20 worth of francs more. Irritated, yet hopeful I will finally have a bed to sleep on, I head wearily back home. When I arrive, our co-renter greets me. She is still convalescing after a motorcycle accident. She "was" living in what is now our house, and was to leave as we arrived. But then, the accident. She needed time to recover. So she lives with us...

Her presence does facilitate my arrival, my integration with this land of never ending enigma. Through her, I forge key links with important African connections. Nonetheless, her extended stay was to last only two weeks... But her contract is somehow extended another four months. Needless to say, compromise, patience, compassion become daily requisites.

It is night. A total darkness flows into our space through the windows. I hear someone walking on the roof of our house. It must be the guard, clearing it of fallen mangoes. His heavy footsteps cause a dog to bark incessantly. To these sounds, my ears add the crowing of rooster. It must be 4 a.m. As I get out of bed, I notice thousands of ants making their way across and down and up and over our kitchen counters. I feel sick to my stomach. Discouraged, I cry. Without realizing it, I am not adapting to this new life, the cadence of it, the rhythm of it. A large fissure is carving itself through my heart.

With the early morning, African life quickly takes wing. And here, life is lived outside. From the rooftop terrace, I notice a neighbour, leaving her house for the well, a large gourd wondrously balanced atop her head. Once this task is completed, she heads out to gather kindling for the morning fire that will soon boil the water. Another neighbour crushes millet for the *To* (traditional African meal), which the whole family shares from the same bowl, each member gathering up handfuls. Older children watch over the younger. Men gather as the local pub radio begins blaring its static fare. Over in another corner, a pig is being bled. There must be a feast somewhere.

I so miss the morning calm of my century-old country home—the one I sold... What has become of it? Seventy-five luscious acres of pristine land whose edges stretch off to the horizon. What of my mountain on that land; the one to whose summit I could climb to my heart's content? And in the evenings, when I would fall deliciously asleep with the sound of our waterfall trickling down to the pond in whose oasis I so loved to swim and linger. Here in Africa, I have difficulty hearing myself think. I miss silence so much.

Adaptation

From the first weeks in Africa, I am like a sponge sucking in all the culture I can, and much of it is time-related. Time in Africa goes by much slower, at a pace that is more human, more relaxed.

This morning I am once again walking to the market. She greets me as she does every day. Ever smiling, she kibitzes with her friends. She is beautiful, attired in her colourful traditional garb. She crosses over to me. We shake hands. She introduces herself. I share a few *Moré* greetings I have learned. From her strong hands, I get several fruit in exchange for 100 francs. There is life, gayety, conviviality in the air. It is Africa at its finest, at its most beautiful.

More than three weeks pass before Ousmane decides to meet with me. As we are alone in my kitchen, he dares speak frankly. Calmly, he explains his vexation at my independent streak. He preferred to let time pass, to have calm return to him before explaining his feelings to me. I had insulted him . . . He had fought to get me a good price at the carpenter's workplace. Why had I not consulted him when things had gone wrong? For my part I had not wanted to trouble him. He sadly responded: "But I thought we had a kinship—both of us on a same trajectory."

This solidarity of purpose and action was foreign to me. I had not developed it in my country since individualism and independence are prized in North America.

Before you Ousmane, I am saddened and ashamed. Before you, I say that I have so much to learn. Not because I have done something wrong, but because our cultures clashed and it is I who must learn yours in your home's.

The neighbour

Night time is here . . . You are at my door, again . . . Yet another visitor. I am flabbergasted and overwhelmed by the constant traffic of visitors, of complaints, of needs. Tonight you are looking for a sponsor, an address, financial assistance for one of your projects. And yet, at the market you constantly ask me for 3 times the price you charge others. You want to leave with me for North America while I have given it up to be here with you. Our identity tags define our differences from which we cannot escape. I come from a rich country and you are from a poor one.

I remain in my room, confronted by a feeling of invasion. Swept clean by a wind of never ending needs, I feel the soil of my soul becoming arid. My indisposition is viewed as bizarre. I am perceived as distant, impolite overly reserved. But in reality, what I am trying to do is to preserve a minimum of space for me to fit in. In fact what I feel is that I now belong to everybody, save myself.

You see... in my land, everyone lives in a private bubble, separate from his or her neighbours and, at times, from his or her own family. There are large treed expanses where no one lives and to where I can escape to listen to the birds near a bubbling brook, to find the calm with which I can recharge my batteries. In your land, you are always with family members. Five children and more sleep in the same space. You share your home with elders while they in turn share their stories and laughter and secrets. You are your very own mutual support system. Family and friends are the core of your being. I admire you. Yet, you and I are so drastically different from each other—both through our origins and our cultures. But ironically, we are similar. We are both children of God; the same one who hears the cry of each of our heart beats and each of our souls; the same, whether called God, Buddha, Allah, Krishna or Great Spirit.

Isolation

Another night . . . The aspirins calm my fever but the stomachache is almost unbearable. The night guard approaches the door, asking: "Is all well, Madame?" Whether I can or not, I must endure the pain until morning when I might have the opportunity to find someone who can help me.

In this total darkness, I fight fear, my insecurities, my mind wanders into dangerous territory. No one is available to either calm my anxieties or deal with my illness. My husband is six hours away, attending a meeting. The house is empty. My mouth is as dry as the desert.

With the morning sun, Florence arrives . . . finally. She finds me rolled into a ball of pain trying to sit up in a living room chair. I am at a loss here . . . without resources, without a tried and true protocol for emergencies. I depend solely on my personal, internal radar, my intuition. But these are insufficient in this environment. My usual calm and determination have shrivelled. I've lost my compass.

I am given the telephone number of Doctor Bounkoungou. I call his cell. "Doctor, can you come visit me. I am truly not well." His answer: "I am approximately 100 km from where you are. I will soon be back in Koudougou and will come as soon as I can."

That same night, I am still suffering. The doctor arrives and soon after my husband who had taken the first bus he could to be back at my bedside. I am calmed by the presence of people around me. Slowly, the feeling of being lost and alone fades.

Communication

In the morning, still in pain, I awake to find my husband busily eating, writing our blog on his computer, then preparing for work. I wonder what he thinks about. We are both at risk here—living the way we are. Once again, he posts a blog entry on our site. I would so love to share my thoughts, the depths of my thinking, my feelings. Mostly, all I want is that our hearts be closer. He leaves. I remain sitting, silent.

After 10 days, my health improves. The numerous tests undertaken find nothing abnormal... And so, I head off to do the work I have created for myself. As is my habit, I greet my colleagues using the few *Moré* words I am capable of. Despite my presence, everyone continues to discuss among themselves in their own language. I feel excluded, isolated. Over and above the language barrier, I am constantly forced to interpret the African "play" on expressions as well as non-verbal communications. Yes means "yes." And sometimes it means "no" or "maybe." I never know what to expect.

These first four months in Africa are made up of incredible discoveries and are filled with serious learning curves. I am from another world. My North American thoughts and communication patterns don't fit here. Everything is an enormous adaptation exercise. I am moved by the humanity of this culture, the lifestyle, the integrated cooperative and supportive nature of the societal structure. And yet I am completely taken aback by the injustices, the contradictions in values, and the constant daily unpredictability of everything. Nothing is what is expected, as if what is expected is nothing.

The shock, created by the huge contrasts encountered, begins to take its toll. The seismic collisions between hopes, aspirations, dreams and reality are much more serious in nature than anticipated. My heart is scarred by a deep, widening trench.

The work dimension (part 1)

My associates

The truth, your truth, rings in my ears. I cringe at the intensity of its impact. "How dare you come to Africa to tell us what to do!"

I feel small, crushed by the weight of this comment. Time freezes. I am here to discuss, "African style" (i.e., in public), what the pertinence of my being here is. Only eight associates from my work group have been invited to attend this gathering presided by the president of the Association.[2] They are all male. My total humiliation before this gathering keeps me silent. I am now intensely aware that I can no longer depend on the support of my colleagues. Even those closest to me bow to the authority of this gathering's stand.

I am in shock. I thought I had followed to the letter the recommendations of my interpreter in order to resolve a work conflict. The atmosphere is tense and uncomfortable. The heat of the day, heavy. Whatever I thought, it is too late. I quickly learn that I should not have taken my concerns to the president but rather to the coordinator. Without knowing it, I had transgressed established rules of engagement in this country: total respect for hierarchy. I am left perplexed by both the complexity of the interpretations brought to my attention and the communication parameters, which to this date remain for me unfathomable.

---

[2] Association pour le Développement des Initiatives de Prévention en Santé / Solidarité

Edouard, the president, tries to calm the situation. He assures everyone that "Elaine has good intentions. She has come to Africa to help us." Tears run freely down my cheeks. I feel an incredible need to disappear, to no longer be present in the proceedings. I am no longer able to control my emotions. There is nothing left to say or do. The meeting ends. I rise from my chair and leave, shutting the door of the office behind me. Alone and crushed, I fall heavily onto the office couch sobbing.

You are right. How pretentious of me to come to Africa like some white knight. You were doing so well before my arrival. How things are done here are certainly different in my eyes. Granted, I have only known North American ways in spite of my previous travels. I would need years of presence and participation in Africa to know even the basics of what and how things must be done. The language, the culture, the multiple nuances dictating actions and expressions and communication... There is so much to learn to integrate, to assimilate.

Despite all of my goodwill and sensitivities, I soon realize that I will be upsetting several individuals along the way—if I am ever to reach a level of accomplishment during my African quest.

Angèle enters the office. She takes me gently into her arms, consoling me. This woman who has lost her husband to AIDS occasionally comes here to the Association. Despite my upset, my embarrassment, my shame, I am calmed by the presence of this angel at my side. We pray together awhile. Reconciled, I can only become through the guidance of a woman—a *Burkinabé* woman who, like me, must accept that this is a world of "men." They dominate and control despite all good intentions of the lesser sex—be it black or white.

The story of Zongo

In your eyes, a deep despair. I can do nothing. You ask questions in need of being asked but for which, sadly, neither I nor anyone else has any answers. Your life story upsets me, crushes me. I so much want to do something—to stifle your immense sadness and worries. I want you to feel that I am here for you. And yet, I too am perplexed and left wondering. I came to Africa, to a great, inspiring people worthy of my awe and respect. And yet . . . within that same collective soul I find so much injustice and rejection.

You are HIV-positive. Having AIDS, you are now being cared for by the Association. Your husband went off to work in the Ivory Coast. He came back a carrier of the disease. He "gave" it to you . . . Last year, he was felled by it and died. As per Burkinabé *custom, upon his passing you become the property of your in-laws as do your 2 children you adore.*

Since your husband's death, you are rejected by his family even though it is within that familial sphere that you must now reside. They accuse you of sorcery, of having been the transmitter of the disease that eventually caused his death. You have no idea whether tonight you will be allowed to sleep upon the small mattress that is yours, or even to see the children for whom you would give your life.

And so it is in this state that I see you now. In your time of loss, you suffer additionally the potential wrenching from you of your own. And this feeling of aloneness increases with every passing day.

Though I do so crave to quench your emotional thirst, to give life-flowing encouragement to your aching heart, I find myself incapable—so damaged and arid my soul has become.

At the monastery

I cry for you now. I cry for your sorrow. I cry that you are being rejected. Your words bring back memories of my own childhood suffering. Having been abandoned by a parent at an early age does leave unseen scars. It causes soul ache. Where I once sought warmth, paternal support, affection, love, all I received was a deep sense of loss, an indescribable sadness. I thought that this wound had long ago healed. Having experienced pain, I thought myself stronger, more able to handle the suffering of others. But I now know that I do not have the strength to protect or even help myself. And so, what now?

Zongo, your suffering has re-opened old wounds. Our discussions haunt me. They fill every corner of my mind and soul. I have great difficulty trying to cope with the return of buried feelings and the symbiosis that has linked us in despair.

To try and deal with all of this, I am off to a nearby monastery for a few days of reflection and rest.

It is a blessing to have found this peaceful harbour. Despite the heavy heat, it is an oasis. Nights are so sweltering, I can hardly sleep. But the gentle days here, blessed with calm, give me rest somehow. Each day, I attend the Benedictine services where the kora and other musical instruments blend with the deep voices in sung prayer. The stressful pressures weighing upon me gradually lift. I begin to ask myself: Am I here for me or am I meant to be at the service of others? Am I deluding myself—to be involved in a humanitarian project?

I had not expected it to be, in so many ways, such a draining experience. Despite a deep felt desire to help those in need, am I equipped to deal with everything I encounter daily? At the same time, am I capable of protecting myself, of being more detached, of dealing with the high levels of stress? Finally, can I manage all of this while tolerating at the same time the emotional over-stimulation caused by an environment hell-bent on careening and crashing into itself?

I am so tired . . . exhausted, demotivated. I have never before encountered such a level of sadness. Will I ever get back my sense of humour, my capacity to laugh, to enjoy and to luxuriate in the beauty that is humanity? Where would I even find this joy while in the midst of all of the suffering and injustice I must face every day? Oddly, I have become numb, incapable of distinguishing what is spiritually and emotionally mine and what belongs to others. And so, depressic sets in.

I am no longer able to assist anybody. I should go, lea·

place. And yet, I don't. I must be loyal to both my husband and the ideals inherent in the work he has undertaken in Burkina Faso. But every day, I am made to confront my worst enemies—a lack of strength, and a feeling of impotence. And so, despite the constant suffering and injustices I am drowning in, I stay.

Helplessness (part 1)

The child

A contagious nausea caused by the smell of urine intermixing with that of death fills whatever space is left in the small room. Your eyes are filled with dread, a gaunt stare of complete horror. You are a mother in distress, in love with and loving your child. And yet some specter spits on, rapes and plunders those feelings.

The ever so minuscule amount of life left in your eyes grasps onto mine, holding them hostage, forcing me to experience the unimaginable sorrow of losing the unimaginable—your child. Your greyed complexion, your bony face are etched in my memory. I would so want to take you tenderly into my embrace, to reassure you and to whisper soft words of encouragement.

And you . . . You who are rigidly immobile, clinging to life by a thread. You are so young. Not yet 2. We've never met, and yet, your eyes reach out despite the gradual melting away of your sweet breath. They reach out to say something. Your lips twitch in silence. And as you fade completely, I sit, staring; wondering what it is that I am supposed to do.

In the bed next to yours is Roumarou.[3] I know him. He too is ill and has been for 2 days now.

Roumarou, who is Florence's four-year-old, is also slowly fading. His skin is gradually turning yellow. As he loses control of his bowels, his mother mops up the flowing urine with her dress. In the public hospital, there is no one assigned to disinfection nor to

---

[3] Florence's son

cleaning. Today there are no doctors in the pediatric ward. I look for a nurse, anyone who can help us. But they are all too busy.

I feel a need to do something quickly. Cubain[4] is still there, standing by the car. I must consult with Soe[5] at the Association infirmary before it is too late.

Soe accepts to come to the emergency public hospital to assess the situation. Seeing the state of the boy Roumarou, she animatedly imparts her analysis of the situation to a nurse. "This boy needs an immediate transfusion!" she barks. But there is no blood in the hospital blood bank. A family member must be found. A cousin is discovered to have Roumarou's blood type. Despite the risk of his blood being contaminated with AIDS, the transfusion process is undertaken.

This is Roumarou's first bout with malaria this year. Nonetheless, despite the emergency transfusion, the four-year-old must spend another night on a ward that is now more reminiscent of a baby cemetery than a recovery room.

The next morning I am back to see how Roumarou is doing. It seems he is gradually regaining his strength and will soon be released to his mother's care. This time, he has survived a serious bout with malaria . . . This time. How things will turn out in the future is another matter.

I turn away to avoid thinking the worst. And there you are . . . still . . . dead. I don't understand. Where is your mother? Where is your father? You have entered another realm alone? With no one accompanying you on this journey?

It seems that your parents had no way of paying for the medication you needed. They are now at home, alone, crying their

---

[4] Driver of the car/colleague
[5] Colleague

incredible loss. The nurses have covered you with a white sheet. They place you in a wheel chair, rolling you by me. Your parents will not come for you. They are ashamed. Forgive them.

I am profoundly moved by this scenario of human misery, by these impossible yet true living conditions, by the lack of government services. I am a witness. Worse, I am an impotent, helpless witness.

Had I known that it was a matter of your parent's inability to pay, I could have taken from my pocket the few francs required to save your life. By the time I discover all of this, it is too late. You are already dead.

Four years have passed since my return to Canada. My poor beautiful child . . . and I am still trying to save you. This evening, you visit me—a ghost from the past. Your spirit still inhabits me. My nightmares reflect my ignorance, my impotence. It's my way of coping with that much too harsh reality, which remains with me to this day. Tonight, I dream I am speeding down the rough road leading to the hospital. Lying across the back seat of the car, you are half alive, half dead, your small person jostled about by the jarring potholes in the road along the way. I desperately search for a doctor to save your life; that life stripped from you; that life stolen from you.

The work dimension (part 2)

Prayer is at the heart of the *Burkinabés*. It is through a deep faith that they find hope, a way of coping with, living with disease and the overall hardships of simply being poor Africans.

Today, a mass is being organized in honour of the sick assembled in the Association office yard. The planning causes many questions to arise within the organization's administration. How is this religious ceremony to meet the collective needs as well as the individual differences of those present? Though they may all be united in suffering, they are nonetheless a mixed gathering of Catholics, Muslims and Animists. More than 50 people in the courtyard are gathered in the silence of their suffering.

The next day Edouard visits me at home. I am visibly discouraged by the situation at work. Following a very frank review of how things are going, he convinces me that the Association both needs and would profit from my talents and experiences.

Initially, I was mandated to be a volunteer, a counselor whose interests would focus on the financial situations in which those living with AIDS find themselves. Personally, I see myself as having reached the limit of my offerings. How am I supposed to support and assist my colleagues at the health café, a project that raises funds for the Association, if there is no openness on his or their part? He resigns himself to redefine my work mandate.

The Association has yet to take on the organization of social activities for the sick. The only thing accomplished so far is a monthly gathering that focuses on educating and where most patients participate simply because a meal is offered to all participants.

Despite serious misgivings, I suggest to Edouard that I could create new activities in collaboration with my African colleagues in order to improve the lives of the sick, to encourage hope and feelings of solidarity among them.

It takes me a few days to get up the courage to actually go to the Association office where I had last been chastised and ridiculed for my innovative ideas. Shoving my ego aside is not easy. Nonetheless, each morning I sit among my colleagues, sharing greetings and asking about their health and that of their families. Their smiles rapidly rid me of my apprehensions. The day goes by quickly and well . . . as if the "reprimand meeting" had never taken place.

The next day, Florent[6] and I are off on an exploratory bicycle trip. We want to know what would give renewed vigor to our beneficiaries; what would make them come alive; what would give them a boost. Based on the gathered information, we would then

---

[6] Colleague

create and organize activities for them.

Sitting between Florent and Adissa,[7] I speak with her—my words interpreted by Florent. Adissa is visibly moved by our interest in her interests. She becomes more and more open to our questions.

After a few weeks into this project, I am more and more enthralled by it. The many visits to the homes of the women increase my awareness of and sensitivity to their situation, which is, more often than not, difficult.

The woman is at the heart of family life in Africa. The children are her responsibility. She also does laundry, grinds the millet, gets the water, prepares the meals and if she has time runs a business in the hopes of making a dollar a day. This amount represents the average salary of an uneducated *Burkinabé*.

Every visit to the Association's sick beneficiaries, mostly widows, must be handled delicately. A visit by a white stranger receives a lot of attention, much of it unwanted. Great care is taken to protect the confidentiality of patients due to the notoriety of the AIDS disease. Organizing each beneficiary visit, therefore, takes time and patience. Most patients benefitting from the Association have neither phone, nor email services. At times, extensive research is required to discover where their homes are. In most quarters, houses have no addresses. A simple visit can take up to five days to plan. Communication is always ambiguous. As stated before, yes can mean yes, no or maybe. A knack for interpreting body language definitely helps.

After a while, the newly organized prayer groups, traditional singing groups and theater completely transform the monthly gatherings. Everything is now livelier, more expressive, more profound. This metamorphosis touches me greatly, giving new worth to my presence in Africa.

---

[7] Beneficiary of the Association

In this country, a great duality exists. On one side, we find the rich interior life of the people and its culture, which serve as food for the soul. On the other side is an intense and relentless daily life. Rare is it that 24 hours pass without something dramatic occurring.

Health (part 1)

My husband's fever is quickly rising again. The medication is not doing its job. I telephone the Association nurse. She agrees to come and help me. As there is no running water in the house, there is no bath. I therefore soak towels in a pail of water. Once soaked I put them in the small freezer we have. My husband smiles when Soe arrives with her medical bag. Soe quickly sets up an intravenous line for the acetaminophen. After an hour, we are all relieved. My husband's temperature is back to normal. Soe leaves, and I am once again alone with my husband.

Not 30 minutes later, the fever is back. I call Soe's cell. No one answers. She must be en route. I am anxious. I run to the house of another nurse. Unconcerned, and even rather blasé, she advises that I give aspirins every four hours. As her door closes, I am panicking. It is Sunday—end of day. The clinic is closed.

At the other end of the line is Conné, our Association coordinator. I need to convince him that I have an emergency. Only through him can I get permission to use the car. I have but an hour before sundown—just enough time to drive 100 km to the Capital. Driving as quickly as I can, my heart is racing. I must focus on avoiding goats and cows on the road. I try to stay calm. This is the first time I drive in Africa. My attentions are divided between my husband who is doing less and less well and the distance still to be covered. On the edge of town, my husband needs to take the wheel. He knows how to get to the private clinic.

The male nurse bellows out: "It's about time you got here. Your husband's fever has hit 40 degrees." Once again, an intravenous connection is made. "We have to keep him overnight to pinpoint the source of his fever," I am told. I spend the night feeling very much alone.

All tests done overnight are inconclusive. The fever source remains a mystery. Despite it having abated, the doctors prefer keeping my husband under surveillance for another night. Everything seems unreal. Exhausted, I am unable to fathom the situation.

Our relationship

My husband's health gets better for a time. But despite the closeness felt during the emergencies, our relationship is somewhat strained. Intimacy is difficult at the best of times. The fault line between us gets wider by the day.

Faced with the everyday challenges of Africa, my ongoing feelings of helplessness and the constant injustices encountered, I increasingly close myself off. I stifle my discomforts while slowly sinking into greater and greater solitude. My husband, on the other hand, turns to rigid logic to justify or explain "what is." More and more, we live in a world of less and less touching, less and less affection, less and less shared emotions.

In Koudougou, there are few venues for entertainment. We therefore occasionally head off to Ouagadougou for a weekend away. Apart from one trip to the capital for a swim in the pool and a visit to a favorite restaurant, two trips to discover more of Burkina Faso and a slice of Mali, nothing much varies our daily routine. There are no opportunities, it seems, to laugh or to maintain the marriage fires. If our relationship was suffering somewhat before our African odyssey, it is certainly at a red light stop at this point. Preoccupied with survival, we seem blind to the situation. How is it possible that we would forget all that time, and despite the obstacles, to simply say the three most important words required: I love you?

Increasingly, I maintain a connection with Soe, my nurse colleague. She makes me laugh and opens up the world of Africa to me in ways that would not have been possible alone. Full of life, she is rather an odd duck in her community. She is educated and has opinions that sometimes clash with the all sacred traditions of her people. I invite her to visit the site of the sacred caymans. Her presence alleviates the constant weight on my shoulders. Her irreverent humour contrasts my melancholy. Nonetheless, the smiles I afford her often hide a desperate need to cry. I am hungry for justice, for stability, for the known, for the comfort that only comes from family that is near. Life in Africa is so, so hard.

A few days following our trek to see the caymans, I notice a change of attitude in Soe. That same evening, she knocks at our door, announcing that her friendship with me is not acceptable to colleagues at work. She is irritated by this turn of events but agrees to submit, saying it's all for the best.

The tension in our house is palatable. Survival is all that gives credence to every new day. I bury myself in the administration of problems. I feel imprisoned—both by the house and the six-foot garden wall. The free space seems to diminish at the same rate as feelings of isolation increase.

The culture (part 1)

I hear the gate creak. Regma[8] is there with his huge smile holding onto his drum. It always brightens up the end of a day. At the same time that I am losing my own beat, I grab onto African rhythms. They help me survive. Music, as always, is my refuge. There are never enough hours in a day to learn the intricacies of the great African drum known as the *djembe*.

As I capture the nuances, I transpose them to paper. I study them. African rhythms are not easy. My structured musical background is a hindrance at times. I must open myself up to the sensual counterpoints of African rhythms. It has been a few months now. And I am slowly becoming one with the beats. Today, I am finally able to follow

---

[8] Musician/young adult orphan

Regma's hands, his beats, his silences and tonal applications of sound bars. When all is somber and heavy within me, I comfort myself in this universal language of heart beats, sensual cadences, sounds of colour and movement.

He dances to the beat of a drum (funerals)

In traditional garb, he dances first for the village chieftain, bare feet, nude torso, to the rhythm of the *kinkané*.[9] In honour of the deceased, several dancers add themselves to the celebration as more and more villagers fill the square. Feasting is in the air.

Bago[10] and I remain watchful. The day is ending, and we have a 10-km motorcycle jaunt to undertake. The time has come to request permission to leave the ceremony. The chief gives us his consent as the spirits show no sign of malevolence. Our trip will be safe and uneventful.

She dances to the drum (the harvest feast)

The road is long, heavy with dust and pockmarked with potholes. Nonetheless, we finally arrive. Cubain introduces me to the Chief who with a nod accepts my presence at the feast. All families from the adjoining villages arrive en masse as the feast to celebrate this year's abundant crop begins. In honour of their revered ancestors, men sit astride 15 foot-long drums, perched a few feet from the ground. Each village proudly displays its own majestic drum. Patiently, the drummers await their time to shine.

The procession begins. I notice her in the crowd. She is barely 12. Though shy, her body sways with the rhythm of the drums. Bare chested, as the tradition demands of all unmarried girls, she dances.

I have difficulty with the leering glances targeting the young girls. I try to hide my discomfort, turning away as best I can. My

---

[9] Musical instrument (small drum)
[10] Colleague

interest in the traditional feasting fades. We leave.

Once home, I head off to a nearby convent where young girls are harboured—girls who run away from home in the hope of avoiding forced marriages.

Polygamy

Florence no longer wishes to live with her family. Nonetheless, her father does not approve of her leaving even an abusive husband. But Florence wishes to see her brothers, sisters and her mother who still live in a remote village. She asks me to come along.

The car is filled to capacity as our Sunday afternoon adventure begins. The road to the village is nearly impassable, and a few times we find ourselves stuck.

Finally at our destination, we are both warmly welcomed by Florence's 70-year-old father, his 7 wives and 40 children. Our arrival coincides with the women preparing the millet from their family garden plot. Each wife has her own mud hut housing her and her children. The last of the wives, in her twenties, is constrained to stay within her hut. As she is only recently married she must stay hidden for a prescribed amount of time.

With much jovial flurry and pride, the father invites us to partake in their meal. Florence giggles as twice he disappears only to reappear in a different fine attire—and this for a family photo. Alongside, his wife and four favored grandchildren.

The visit is pleasant and filled with humour. Before leaving, the host patriarch addresses me in a very charming manner. Florence displays a wide teasing smile as she translates his most unforgettable words: "My father would like to know if you would be so gracious as to accept to become his ninth wife." I burst into laughter saying: "A white wife??? That's way too much to have to deal with!" On the way home Florence and I fill the air with laughter.

I dance to the sound of drums

Tonight, all the locals are assembled in the courtyard of a small hut. Their souls are filled with boisterous laughter. A chicken, its head gone, bloody, still alive, runs wildly between my legs. The blood of the sacrificed animals is poured before the hut of the priestess. The welcome I am afforded is doubly impressive as I am told the ancestors bless my presence at this ceremony to cure the ills of the sick.

The men beat relentlessly their drums. The sick eat, sleep, and dance for three days in the hope that the ancestors will bless them with a cure.

While the fragrant meat cooks atop an outdoor fire, the women gather. The sound of their maracas blends with the drum rhythms. They invite me to their ritual. We encircle the priestess endowed by the ancestors to cure. With short soft steps we dance.

With darkness enveloping us all, the priestess pulls me into the centre of the dance circle. She hands me a horse tail whip. She indicates I should whip the tail while the women sing, encircling me. With the power of drumming and moving rhythms entrancing, my head twirls as I gradually sink into a quasi-drunken state that lasts the whole evening.

Slowly, gently, throughout the night, the spirit of the ancestors leaves my tormented soul. Will they be back to haunt me again? Is my presence at this most sacred ceremony truly welcomed by all?

Helplessness (part 2)

Clarisse

In Burkina Faso, I am constantly bound to two extremes, two opposite poles: at one end the rich and moving cultural attributes while at the other the daily difficulties, haunts and injustices.

No one is indifferent to Clarisse, the eight-year-old orphan. She walks the eight kilometers between her village and the dispensary, barefoot, accompanied by her aging aunt. She comes to consult with the doctor. Her eyes say it all. The melancholy is palpable. Her abdomen is distended, her once joyous laughter replaced with a heavy silence. My husband cannot do enough to save her. Sadly, her visits neither bring about light at the end of a tunnel nor any other form of hope. She is soon taken from us—our clinic not being equipped to treat children with AIDS.

A car transporting her back to her village stops at our house. Clarisse's small frame lies on the back seat cradled by her old aunt. My husband goes out to say his goodbyes. I am called. It is my turn. I freeze . . . I am unable to leave my room. I can't seem to feel for fear of breaking down completely. The car slowly rolls away along the rutted road to the village.

If only we had danced for her, would the ancestors have answered our prayers?

Health (part 2)

For the last six months of our stay in Africa, maintaining my health becomes a daily challenge. Mosquitoes abound during the rainy season. My fear of malaria is heightened.

Despite all the precautions, the fly swatter, the window screens, the mosquito netting over the bed, there always seems to be a small specimen invading my shower. The medication I am taking, Lariam or Mefloquine, protects us from three of the four types of malaria. In fact this medication actually masks the symptoms of the fourth type. No one escapes this dreaded disease.

I am eventually struck by a mild form of malaria along with bronchitis and this mix three times over. But despite the smaller infection, malaria kills if it is not treated immediately. It attacks the system making a patient weak and tired. To walk from the bed to the toilet is a trying exercise. Gradually, resilience being effected, the afflicted becomes less and less able to stand up to the attacks.

Between each recovery, a series of clinic visits is required. At first, I am felled by violent abdominal cramps. Blood tests reveal I am infected by an *E. coli* bacteria. I am therefore hospitalized for 24 hours. Despite these challenges, I am warmly moved by visits from colleagues and from Regma. Such support and encouragement is a by-product of a cultural recognition of the other—except in the cases of AIDS where shunning is a more revealing form of recognition.

From one week to another, I take in all forms of medication. The heat, always the heat, becomes unbearable—thermometers often displaying 45 degrees Celsius. The sensations are similar to sitting too close to an outdoor bonfire from which you are unable to step back. Seeking a bit of but never finding fresh air becomes the daytime nightmare de rigueur. Whether outdoors or in, the stifling heat is the same suffocating phenomenon.

In order to get any work done, I must confine myself to the bedroom, which has a primitive form of air-conditioning. But Mother Nature has no pity. After the dry season of heat, there is the windy season that whips up sand and dust in a suffocating mix of lung damage. And with that other forms of sickness rise.

Please, Doctor, come quickly!

My digestive system is completely out of whack. My intestines are totally blocked. I sit on the toilet seat completely dilated, yet nothing flows. Naked, lying face down on the tiled shower floor, I scream a horrible scream. My husband tries to soften the feces using a syringe filled with warm water. For the next eight hours the pain is excruciating. I feel faint and afraid I will never wake. My whole weakened body is racked with pain.

I don't remember how I got to the car. It is early morning, yet the sun already beats down unmercifully. My garden is nothing more than a weed bed.

Stretched out on the clinic bed, I wait for the doctor. He has been called in from home. Eyes closed, I pray I will see my family and friends once again.

The digital scraping required is without a doubt the most painful experience of my life. Despite all the care possible, my endless screams can be heard all the way to the waiting room.

The culture (part 2)

With the passing days, my health improves. In lapses strength returns and, eventually, I am able to venture out on a cultural visit. These rare outings seem to be the only kindling that fire up my will to go on. During the Atypical Koudougou Night festival, it is thrilling to discover the presence of musicians from everywhere—Niger, Togo and Mali. How wondrous it is to see the *Burkinabé* youth dancing with such agility and power. I think: "For such few pleasures . . . such pain."

The artisan

Attending the Regional Festival of African Artisans, I wander about from tent to tent. What talent is displayed. They have come from all parts of the land. A wide array of quality craftsmanship proudly shines: silver jewelry, leather sandals, masks and traditional yard goods. The stalls are filled and varied.

I enter your tent to study the fine jewelry. Our eyes meet. A shiver passes through me. Out of curiosity I ask the price of a piece . . . I can't seem to escape your stare. Where I go you are there. I feel chased. You seem to follow me everywhere—a piece of jewelry in hand and a tone of desperation in your voice. Despite the incomprehensible dialect spoken I am increasingly discomforted by the insistence that I buy. I say no thank you and move on. Obstinate you persist. You are now too near to me. You yell and demand and press for a sale. A feeling of vulnerability overwhelms me.

People gather, worried, encircling us. As your insistence is becoming worrisome, I look around me. No policemen are available. You touch me, push me. My husband appears, and you back off faced with the presence of a man. My heart beats faster and faster for the longest while as I hurry off away from the festival.

Health (part 3)

My husband is not well. Headaches, grating cough and fatigue. He heads off to the local dispensary to be tested. The parasite count is high. It is urgent that malaria treatment starts now.

From one day to the next, I live in agonizing fear. The symptoms quickly escalate. I insist we go to the clinic for further consultation. As I look upon him laid out exhausted on the hospital bed, I experience a rushing fear that I will lose my partner. My heart rate rises. In the small room we suffocate—the heat oppressive, overwhelming. A nurse begins to attend as the doctor announces that pneumonia is attacking both his lungs.

I remember little if anything of the passing days. Only the feelings of helplessness and fear remain. Without thought or concentration, I simply go about doing whatever it is I must do. Remembering much of that time is difficult except that I know things could have gone seriously worse. What my mind could not analyze, the body nonetheless absorbed. And for years it remained frozen and festering, fed by a state of endless fear and sadness.

The orphanage

Here in Africa, it is stated that "the drink we never tire of is water, the fruit of which we are never weary is the child."

Children are so candid in Africa; so full of life. Their presence is a gentle pleasure, which counterbalances the constant threats of death, the omnipresence of life ending.

Once a week, I bicycle to the orphanage, which stands at the rim of Koudougou. It is a 40-minute ride. A thread of sanity is woven tightly between the children and I. Regma, especially, remains to this day a part of me. We still talk to each other via email.

With the passing of days, I question the validity, the value of my presence in Africa. I came to help, but I often have the impression that I receive more than I am giving. The cooperation between we foreign associates and the *Burkinabés* is precious—an incredible learning experience. I discover in these people values that capitalist societies have summarily abandoned. Each encounter brings me to the discovery of what is at the heart of African survival: patience, resilience, tolerance, agility, humour, deeply felt welcomes, warmth, sharing, generosity and solidarity.

The hospital

All of my team-workers are at the hospital. Every task has been abandoned for the sake of assisting one of our colleagues who has had a motorcycle accident. He is lying on a hospital bed, bleeding profusely, and yet the nurses refuse first aid. Strange! There is no medical equipment in sight. No gloves, no gauze, no antiseptic. Nothing but a pen and paper with which they create a list of first aid equipment required. Everyone searches their pockets for money, loose change, anything. After three hours pass, the required medical supplies arrive. Had the injuries been life-threatening, he would never have made it.

My soul's eyes are opened wide by this experience. It still haunts me. The day before, I had visited the capital. I saw the President's mansion. It is larger than our own Prime Minister's residence. Taking pictures is forbidden . . . There is no doubt in my mind that needed medical supplies, hospital equipment—nothing is made available despite governmental promises. No money reaches the poorest of the poor. That the consequences of abused privilege could so openly bleed before me flabbergasts.

I am but a grain of sand lost in a vast desert ocean of injustice compounded by my impotence.

Chapter 3: Returning Home

December 2006

I have fallen asleep; my packed bags strewn about near the bed. I am startled by Angèle who raps loudly at the door. I had not properly set my alarm. The long journey to the airport is strained. The airport porters overwhelm me with their offers of service. I lose patience, become irritated. Luckily, the plane to Canada is late. But still, the goodbyes are said too quickly.

Arriving in Canada with our multiple bags, I am startled by the contrasts. My lungs are shocked as I step outside for a breath of fresh air. My body has forgotten the sensation brought on by a sudden freezing cold. And it is this sensation, this cold, which, penetrating to the greatest depths of me, renders me frozen—emotionless.

Café au lait

On our first morning back, my husband and I sit in a restaurant. We take in the smell of fresh coffee. For 10 months now I have been dreaming of smelling and tasting fresh ground coffee. My stomach growls with impatience. Everything seems surreal. From the first steps on home soil, I have the impression of having escaped from the grasp of one of the poorest countries in the world to the embrace of a fairyland. I read the menu aloud. Each item seems to have an aura of grande-cuisine about it. And the offerings? They appear endless. Wow! Everything I encounter fascinates me. I am like a child suddenly discovering the wonders of the earth: the smells, the tastes, the holiday decorations. Then there are the people, their attitudes, their silences, their greetings. I am a stranger in my own land as I dig into a syrupy crepe overflowing with luscious fruit.

Despite my illness-ravaged body systems, my first month in Canada becomes one of decadence and exaggeration. I escape into a world of excesses in food and drink and shopping and feasting.

To those who ask about our adventure, I weave a tapestry of vast learned riches and equally great difficulties and yet... I avoid truthful recollections of what "really" happened. I do feel the empathy displayed and serious interest in our experiences, but I fail to click with this newly reacquired environment with which I suddenly feel incapable of re-connecting. And since I am not being honest on the telling of the truth, no one seems to notice the disconnect growing within me.

Despite the pleasure of once again being with family and friends, that disconnect becomes a feeling of vulnerability, of helplessness.

I come to fear being alone. I need contact 24 hours a day. My imagination often goes into overdrive. And when African musical sounds reverberate, I see faces and smiles. It is the African children I miss. Yves, Georges, the beautiful Nadisse, and most especially Regma and his wondrous smile. My heart hovers over two worlds and fears the eventual landing.

The great void

There are grey clouds on the horizon. A storm is coming. The honeymoon ends as a great void begins to take up more and more space in my heart. I am overwhelmed by a feeling of vertigo, of falling into a deep dark depth. I can't control the intensity of my emotions. A loud scream wants to pierce the walls of the vacuum I have become. All I can think is: "Holy shit!"

I find a pair of boots from the strewn boxes in our apartment. I need air and rush off into the winter at a wild pace. I run and run, but my weakened state stops me. I am breathless. My batteries are dead. I have no reserve energy. Psychologically, I lose the thread in all of this dark emptiness. And that's when I discover in me an overwhelming fear; a desperate holding onto nothing. Nothing!

Despite the rediscovered comfort so richly available in my country, everything is strange. I recognize my clothing and my *djembé*. But everything else is a blur. I have no place, no home; nowhere to be. These books, cooking pots, that painting, this divan, nothing is mine in this rented apartment. Lost, nomadic in a quest to reach nowhere, I wander the streets of Old Hull, Quebec; searching for a viable direction. For a moment, I find solace in lightly falling snow flakes, resting gently on my hair, caressing oh so softly my cheeks.

I return to the apartment. I am tired and wish to dream of a better tomorrow. My husband is there. He sleeps. He too is between states. Like me he is still travelling, wandering; being not here nor there. Finally, I find rest cuddled up by his side.

The next morning I awake suddenly, needing to run. I am suffocating. I punch the key into the ignition and drive off, music blaring. Go! Run! Forget!

The instability

My husband and I walk the Centretown streets in Ottawa, Ontario, looking for a new rental apartment. My anxieties are beginning to take over. I don't understand them. I have difficulty breathing.

Back in Hull, across the bridge from Ottawa, I again feel suffocated. Friends leave me their place for two weeks while they are away. I feel a strong need to be alone, to sort things out, away from my husband. Secretly, I invite a friend. The meeting with this kindred spirit overpowers as I suddenly feel a tearing apart, a rending of the heart.

This passionate affair, this meeting of souls takes me out of myself and away from my torment. I grab onto its intensity, which temporarily protects me from the deep dark hole that constantly threatens to engulf me. For a moment in time I forget I am lost; at sea without a compass.

I don't understand this sudden total indifference, this throwing away of 10 years of marriage. He asks me . . . I admit it. He is deeply hurt. I had never before cheated on him.

I no longer, it seems, believe in God or in marriage. My values are out of whack. I've lost it. I do not recognize myself.

I have lived among those who daily suffer most on the planet. I was near death. And now, I am incapable of projecting myself into the future or even able to imagine what "future" actually means.

A weird sensation overtakes me. I feel like I could die at any moment. And because of that, all I want to do is live to the fullest—bite into life with total abandon; without restraint or societal convention.

I no longer belong here. The values I encounter every day are no longer mine. Connecting the dots between African values and capitalist ones is an impossibility. I've lost my identity, my direction, my soul. In Africa, I knew of what importance I was. People turned to me for assistance. Here, I am nothing. Nobody.

Three months back home and I am an even greater stranger to others and to myself than I was in Africa. A debriefing session is planned by our non-profit organization. It has come too late. Why now? I refuse to be a part of it. I refuse to let go of my new found obsession with living to the fullest. Lose a day to debriefing? Never! I would rather fill my time with enjoyment—and that, into the hours of the mornings.

Finally, what I am doing is avoiding and compensating. It's better than the nothing I find myself increasingly falling into.

I am disillusioned. My husband, my once best friend sits before me. In vain he attempts a reconciliation. I am unable to feel love. With each of our meetings, all I re-experience is suffering, Africa and emptiness.

Would it not be worth it to try to rekindle the fires of our marriage? But then, how can I go back to a "once was" when there is nothing there to resurrect? What is it with this indifference?

To flee the breakup, this despair, this blackness, I am now in an apartment alone. And alone I fall and fear. When I leave this havenless haven, I am forever taking one step forward, ten back. I live with constant devastating setbacks. I lose myself in vulgarity; broken, fragmented, smashed.

The Divorce

May 23, 2008, is the anniversary of our 10th year of married life. I have difficulty taking in the lawyer's words . . . She confirms it. We are divorced. It matters not that I was the instigator of both the separation and the final decree.

I am alone. In a fetal position, my suitcases once again strewn about and around me. I cry and scream. But nothing stops the hurt, the pain, the sorrow. All so overwhelming, I feel as if I will regurgitate my insides. I have lost everything.

During our last meeting, my husband announces he is pursuing more studies and a career in international mediation. He leaves for Africa once again. But this time it is to the Congo—a country where violence reigns. My heart is in shreds. Even though I am in a relationship with another man, I still have feelings for my husband. It takes everything I have to not object, to not interfere with his plans. I need to let him go.

The mourning period after the death of a marriage is long and difficult. The first month, filled with anxiety, distress and heavy feelings of guilt, almost drowns me. Depression strikes and suicidal thoughts fill my days and nights. That I hold onto life is a matter of grasping at a very thin thread.

The fears encountered revolve around my husband dying in Africa. Despite the consequences, I take on the guilt and responsibility for his departure, for his life. If I had not left him, would he have gone off to this even worse part of the world?

For months, he is the subject of my nightmares. Tonight, I see him again. This time, a gun to his head, finger on the trigger . . . I awaken startled, sweating, gasping for breath. Endless tears cover my lover's chest as he calms me, reassures me, loves me.

My heart is rent in several places. The first caused by sadness, the second through impotence and the third through guilt. For three years, these eat away at me like a spreading cancer of the soul.

Chapter 4: The Diagnosis

The three lacerations tormenting my heart are seriously destructive. Despite all the efforts to rid myself of them, they are more and more effective in destabilizing me. The sadness, this feeling of inability, this guilt rips apart my mind, my heart, my soul. I am constantly anxious. Crying becomes a daily habit. From time to time, in odd quiet moments when there are no feelings felt, the tears simply fall. Why? Sometimes I have no idea. They just do.

Every day, the anxieties rise with the sun. They are with me at work and stay with me during meals and until sleep overtakes. Try as I might, I cannot control them. They stifle. They strangle. I cannot hide anywhere. I try a different tact—understanding them, treating them through naturopathy. Nothing helps. Daily, I find an increase in worry, fear, loss. There are not enough hours in a day to contain them. With no respite, I do not see the storm coming.

A year after the divorce, I crumble. With depression broad-siding any and all efforts, I am forced to stop working for two months. The doctor fears I am trying too hard to return to work. He fears an even more serious relapse. But in my mind being replaced at work, losing all financial security is not an option. I must try to get back to "normal." After a couple of weeks into a regular routine, wishing that all will be well, the anxieties dig themselves out of their much too early grave and once again haunt my every hour.

The catalyst

June 2010

I sit in your office, staring at you. Your lips move but I don't hear anything they say. Behind the protective wall I have erected, a rage is slowly rising. It is only with the greatest difficulty that I don't explode. Seconds pass like hours—slowly, ever so slowly. My ship is sinking. I am sinking. I now see it, feel it... I am ill and I am drowning in that illness.

Whatever goodness or sensitivity you may have within you, it is invisible. Within the cold shell I perceive before me, I am blind to whatever benevolence, whatever kindness you may feel toward me. Any strength, any comprehension I may have had before this moment leaves my body. Torn, I want to understand your position, your needs. But I can't. I desperately must protect myself, respect whatever integrity is left in me. You are the authority, the employer. You have the power. I . . . ? I am nothing but the epitome of weakness.

I don't remember leaving your office. I don't remember driving to my psychologist's office. But I know that it has taken every ounce of energy to get me there. More and more, a paralysis enveloped in darkness is closing in. And it comes as no surprise that within the following two-week period, I am medically diagnosed as suffering from post-traumatic stress disorder and depression.

With this news whirling at hurricane speed inside my head, I finally make it home and crash. The tears flow beyond any natural capacity. I am devastated. For the past five years I have dedicated myself to accompanying those who are sick and dying. My work is more a vocation than a job. It is inspirational. The creativity required refreshes me. It is the only venue of happiness I have. It is the only arena in which I can exercise the skills I have developed over 20 years. And now . . .

With the weight of this diagnosis I suddenly realize that from the day I left for Africa, my fate had been sealed. My precious house and land are lost, my marriage is gone, and now, a cherished career. With nothing before me, I am the one who is lost and afraid. In this greatest of turmoils, I envision only a deep dark hole.

The boss

At night, you are part of my dreams. You ask me to pull back, to stop collaborating with certain people with whom I have been working daily. This, you say, is for a better work-result ratio. You see my being friendly and open with everybody as not being professional. I feel spied upon, shoved aside. And, inevitably, what I fear most happens: I am completely isolated, made to work alone—to not be a part of the team whose goals were once mine.

Slowly some of my administrative responsibilities are taken from me. You assert your authority in front of my patients and colleagues. I am humiliated and it does not seem to matter to you that I am . . . You belittle my past experiences. You reject my opinions and my approach to problem solving. And now, attaining the level of excellence I seek is nigh impossible. Is it the goal of the administration to rid themselves of me? If so, I can't take much more . . . I sense a going off of the deep end. In a sweat, I awaken; frightened, gasping.

Though I need the regenerative powers of sleep, I find it difficult to rest. My mind does not stop wandering and wondering. Is my illness affecting work performance? Are the perceptions scrutinizing me factual? Are the actions being taken by the administration just? On and on and on my mind whirls faster and faster. And once again, I jump from a distraught semi-sleep into a state of anxiety. The sheets, wet with sweat, are clammy to the touch as my heart sinks ever deeper into a never before known despair.

My every new day is difficult to face. Tainted by the nights of incessant nightmares, I lose confidence in my ability to do anything. My integrity has not only been questioned, it has been crushed and finding the leftover scraps is a daunting task.

Post-traumatic stress disorder: a psychological and spiritual wound

Disabled by this incomprehensible and overwhelming diagnosis, I walk about in a daze. Survival is the destination, but the way there is unknown. Both financially and emotionally, I am paralyzed. Thoughts of Africa haunt me. And when they repeatedly do, I find myself falling ever deeper into a dark hole from which I don't think I can extricate myself. And all the while I am no longer part of either my body or soul. Anxieties and anger rise with each passing moment, each trial interaction. I try to make heads or heels out of everything but it is too much. It all spins out of control.

Though I scream, there is no sound. Though I beg desperately to be heard, no one sees nor hears me. And yet, all the while horribly painful sobs overwhelm my whole being.

Suddenly, relationships are impossible. Beginnings and endings are too painful, and so there are none anymore. Both spiritually and emotionally, I am numb. I am a bodiless soul riddled with an incurable cancer.

Cut off from reality as everyone else knows it to be; cut off from my own emotions, I feel disconnected from tenderness, affection, love. They are like meaningless clouds hovering at heart level—passing through with no ill or good effect. I've become dehumanized, cold, disassociated. Fragmented, I am a smashed mirror whose sharp cutting shards litter my own and everyone else's path. If I had always dreamed of discovering a world of justice, peace and harmony, I now feel nothing. And as the battle within me rages . . . a mix of vile coarseness, sadness, anxiety and guilt gouge the very sheath that protects that soul of mine. For all intents and purposes I no longer give a damn.

As long as a soul is in revolt, there is palpable hope. But abused, a soul quickly becomes de-sensitized and even catatonic. And that is what it is like to be disillusioned, lost, depressed.

An indentation forms. A massive footprint imposes itself on my face and breasts and pelvis, legs and arms. Like an invisible scarring, I am tattooed by fear. Jean-Paul Mari, author of the book *Sans blessures apparentes* (*No Visible Scars*) summarizes this phenomenon well. "Having experienced death is to have its recall settle like a black diamond on the surface of the brain. Immovable, it nests there, rising imperceptibly." Images, odors, sounds . . . They are stamped upon my memory with such force that I reel at their unsolicited recall . . . every night for months on end.

Time has lost its essence as a tape runs endlessly through my mind; playing unrelenting, intrusive, obsessive thoughts. Each day becomes the nightmares I suffer through each night. Increasingly, I am transported into a nether world of helplessness. I become chronically irritated and irritating. I am hyper-alert, anxious, ever on guard for threats real and imagined. Concentrating on any one theme is impossible. My memory is erratic and emotions raw and unpredictable.

My wound is physical in that I am rendered frozen. I am afraid; locked up by my own unintelligible emotions.

And yet, despite the never ending ache, I avoid suicide despite its constant siren call. Ironically, I refuse its luring gait, its bliss-filled curse for one reason and one reason only. The excruciating pain it would cause my family reminds me that those feelings I am enduring are nothing in comparison to theirs at the discovery of my deed.

At the best of times, I remind myself that the damned post-traumatic stress disorder is a normal reaction to an abnormal situation. For a while, this is enough to ward off the ever encroaching feelings of shame and guilt.

As the lucid moments make themselves rare, I grab onto any and all of them. Every logical moment is required. I need to be pressed into a war against this scourge, this cancer afflicting my soul. I need to become my own general to dive head-on into the heart of my suffering. I need to put words to the tangible pain I am suffering. But to interpret, to redefine and to render clear those words, I need an advisor, a professional who can free both the emotions and the answers.

Diagnosed three years after returning to Canada from Africa, my illness is now more complex and now more difficult to treat. Generally, post-traumatic stress disorder (PTSD) manifests itself a few months after an initial trigger. The therapy I undertake is rough as, one after the other, traumatic episodes reveal themselves.

From the beginning, everything undertaken is blurry, incomprehensible to me. For all intents and purposes, I am literally absent from the reality of it all—my troubles, the triggers, my life, the lives of others. The whole concept is one day at a time, one minute at a time. I am in survival mode without knowing it. But with feelings coming back into the picture, I find myself picking up a pen—reconnecting with words. I write a few lines—just a few at a time. Sitting at the piano I find myself unable to read the notes. And so I play whatever. I let it flow. And a bit at a time, I begin to give voice to my emotions. The most significant tools in this process of recovery are this writing that I am scribbling out of me, this note playing. From here on in, it is heart and soul recovery time. Reconciliation begins with the person in the mirror.

Chapter 5: The Road to Recovery

Year 2010

September 2010

I am nothing more than a shell of what I once was. My eyes no longer see nor wish to see. There is no life in my soul. I feel incapable of loving or being loved. And in this state of nothingness, I lose the will to live.

Shame

The greatest enemy in this war to regain balance is my fear—the fear of being judged, rejected, blamed. My biggest secret: shame. But what is shame? A feeling of having failed? A feeling of "I should have known—known better, known more"? A feeling of having followed another's dream, another's intuition and not my own? Is this shame a consequence of fears, of withheld anger, of aggressive feelings towards myself—towards others?

The comfort I crave is to allow myself the right, the power to speak, to open up, to say it the way it is—the way I have felt it and lived it. I need to be genuine with others, with myself. The time for truth is now. But for the moment, I am far from being able to deal with the immensity of it all. Isolating myself, I avoid what I want most—to communicate with or confront anybody. I don't recognize this person I am. And so, I hide in the darkness of my soul.

Humility

The receptionist

You stare at me, perplexed. You're waiting for an answer—my telephone number. Tears fall. They highlight my shame and veil my frowning features. I can't remember the numbers. Anxiety strangles me. I need to leave this space—get a breath of fresh air. After a while I return to the waiting room. In the hall, a silent television screen promotes nothing and everything; selling its wares to no one and everyone. I stare at the monitor, seeing only a reality TV shtick of slides reviewing my past.

The friend

Back within the protective space of my apartment, the phone rings. I see your number on the caller ID and I tell myself that I will call back when I am better . . . I know that you are calling just to see how things are. You haven't seen me for a while. Several days pass without me calling you. You're worried. You come over for coffee. I am happy to see you. You're my friend. For your presence, I am grateful.

We talk. And suddenly you ask: "Are you OK?" My eyes wander, fixated on nothing and everything. I can't seem to concentrate, to create, to compose cohesive sentences, to express ideas or feelings. I've hit a brick wall . . . I silently lie across the couch. You stay with me.

The partner

My partner enters our home. Despite a full afternoon of rest, I am exhausted. Preparing the evening meal becomes an almost impossible chore. He sidles up—kisses me. I am startled at the sudden tenderness. His eyes are loving. He looks for the same in mine. But though I am present—here with him in body, my soul is in another world. Only pain is present. My heart is not. He embraces me lovingly and for a second or so I sink heavily into him. Again, his eyes seek me out, loving . . . I am not there.

The child

The evening light fades, darkens, blackens. Frantically, erratically, I drive the old car; pointing it in any and every direction a hospital might be. My heart races. In the last throes of the day's heat, sweat slides, cools my stomach. You? You lie silent on the back seat, hovering between the last of life's breaths and death. I look over fearful. Your eyes stare back, digging into me.

Startled, I jump. The sheets fly off and, away from me... My breathing is deep and erratic. Another nightmare. As always, I can only lay back, sweat dampened, trembling, wishing for another better day, better night, better day...

You are a child. You are an adult. You are my friend, my family, a stranger, a neighbour. Before you I appear whole. But hidden within is a scar deeply gouging whatever is left of what and who I am. Before you, I wander about ashamed.

Medical treatment

I resign myself to the inevitable—taking meds. I've tried everything to avoid them. I've tried everything from the obvious to the most innocuous—from homeopathy to healers. I did feel, I think, some light improvement from the application of creams and other wild plant based concoctions. But the effects were always fleeting—much like my wishes that everything be better.

Being medicated is a last resort. I submit to taking them because they allow me to exit that dark hole in which I am drowning. Because of them I can somewhat function. I am well-aware they are a crutch. But something has to hold me up, otherwise...

Anti-depressants give me a certain aloofness—a space in which to breathe deeply. I feel detached, less reactive to everything around me. I am able to consider and analyze better with them. They permit me to better negotiate life, to somehow better avoid the crashes I constantly fear. For all intents and purposes, the medication is necessary if I am ever to get better. To live with, to face PTSD along with the depression accompanying it, I bow to the superior authority of medication—at least for now. Encouragingly, my doctor and my psychologist never give up on me or my tomorrows. They constantly repeat that I will overcome what seems to me impossible—that I will win each battle one day at a time. And though I don't see this, I feel blessed that someone does.

Unable to fathom what is relentlessly hitting and punching me I am given the analogy of PTSD as diabetes. I am made to understand that a diabetic needs medication to balance the sugar in their blood as a sufferer of PTSD or depression needs meds to balance the "imbalance" in their brain. I am lucky. I meet a psychiatrist who knows well what I am dealing with and who can recommend the right medications in the doses required.

As days pass and crash, therapy becomes primordial, basic, fundamental. The flashbacks are too intense, too overpowering. They block any and all exits from the never ending fears and anxieties being encountered. I feel cornered, cowed, too behaviourally restricted to function normally. My psychologist becomes my "gardener." She tends to my soul growth despite an environment of strangling weeds and lifeless earth. She is an indispensable part of my recovery. Well qualified, she is also warm, respectful and eminently professional. And these are essential elements for someone to accompany another someone in this journey of discovery and recovery. She seems to know which of my life plants are weeds and those which are not—which to nurture and which to extract. With encouragement, I eventually, slowly, begin to try some of the nurturing, some of the extractions on my own.

My psychologist recommends eye movement desensitization and reprocessing (EMDR). By some, it is considered being hypnotized while being awake. I am formally but gently instructed on the details of this procedure. It entails recall and this can be and is difficult for me. But remembering, and allowing the hurts are requirements for the transformation to begin. Without any other recourse or viable direction other than that being offered, I agree . . . hesitantly. The first months of this new tactic are intense. I often leave the sessions pale and exhausted. Driving home on my own is at times impossible. Over and above feeling drained after each session, the process is time-consuming. However, the intensity and devastation of experiences recalled eventually diminish. The changes encountered and the relief, though slow coming, are progressive and lasting.

The past

Sitting on the edge of Amik Lake, I cry my husband lost. I cry for me; for the separation. I cry the hurts we inflicted upon each other. I cry for his pain and for mine. I thought I had already cried all of this out of my system, but I was wrong. Thirsty for a refreshing waft of peaceful breezes we once shared, I walk forest paths we once walked. I feel him there despite the distances separating us and the time that gradually erases our being together.

I remember his energy, the smiles, the dreams. I want to caress his hair in remembrance of our ten years of making each other both sad and happy. I recall the illnesses and near deaths we faced. Because of all of this we remain linked.

Overcoming discouragement

Though reconfiguring, reassigning and redefining myself is in the works, I am, for now, in a day to day survival mode. I ask for no more. Nonetheless, the disconcerting gradual realignment of my person is already rendering more tangible a perception of the new "me." And with this, the old self gradually fades . . .

Staring at the mirror, I realize that my illness is there but invisible. My only tangible consolation is the road travelled. On first reflection, I focus on my limitations. But then I note that self-respect is not possible if I only recognize where I have been. I must also accept and respect where I am and where I am going. And so, before offering up to the world a visible me again, I need to take in and take on the whole of me and every aspect of my unique history. The re-becoming of a confident "me" demands it.

Despite any and all apprehensions, I push myself to increasingly encounter, meet with and confront others. But these taking-charge moments are never as difficult as meeting, encountering, confronting and directly facing the reality that is my PTSD.

Nonetheless, it is always difficult to leave the sanctuary, the safe haven that is my home. The fright of exposing myself; my vulnerability to others, is overwhelming. The constant battle between the desire to isolate the frightened me—a feeling that I should just lie on my couch and wait—and the determination to heal is intense. The power of it exacts its toll—a great tiredness—both emotional and physical. It is only through sheer determination that I push myself into action, expending the energy required to take the first steps that get me moving forward. And for that to be possible, I depend heavily on a regular exercise program, which releases endorphins in the brain and counteracts the depressive symptoms.

The stranger

The day is warm and inviting. Even before setting out on bicycle, I sense the coolness of a breeze. I am eager to get out, to feel the well-being of movement, the song of birds entertaining me.

I make a short detour to the bank. I bring the bike into the building. You follow me in—to transact your own banking requirements. And suddenly you hit where it hurts. "Some people are afraid their bikes will leave before they do? Some people certainly thrive on negative thinking." I try to not let your joke, your mocking tone affect me. Nonetheless, I can't help but react. Why am I so touched by this ordinary event—this banal try at humour?

Since the return from Africa, I find myself locking everything, trusting no one. I am wary of strangers. Frozen in an ever-hovering fear, I am afraid of thieves, of being harassed. But this, you do not see . . . as I continue on my way; as I leave the bank and go off on my bike ride.

Home again, I read an article describing the life of a retired policeman. As it was during his days as an officer, he still has a partner. But now, it is a dog— a special animal trained to help those who suffer from PTSD. The man explains how his dog helps him when he is disoriented or needs to get away from a public place when anxiety strikes. The dog knows his car, knows how to physically push an automatic door latch or bark for assistance (*www.canineswithacause.org*).

Over and above the help given, the dog is a companion, a stress monitor when his master needs to leave the house. I dream of a helper, a stress companion.

Year 2011

Life after death

Spring 2011

I am suddenly reborn—if only precariously. Rediscovering what it is to be "thrilled," I am seeing the world anew; allowing myself to be awed by images, sounds, smells. Amazed by all that is before me, I step down from my bicycle. I stop to simply take in the moment. Not far away, a horse stares; his mane dancing gently in the breeze. I hear another galloping in the fields. A cardinal joyfully adds melody to the silence. Tears fall warmly, gently, while I gaze at a world more welcoming and beautiful than I was ever able to recognize before this day.

In this state of grace, I realize that my affliction is a blessing, not a curse. I have been given the opportunity to compare . . . to savour life fully through the rich gift of its simplicity. And to realize I am actually a part of all of this is overwhelmingly calming.

Living fragile

Well turned out, a smile on my face, calm, I exude an image of someone in the best of health . . . My wounds are invisible to others. Much as a child learning to walk, I practice the steps that assure me balance, solid footing. Some areas are safer than others. I learn to discern which are which. Some environments for some reason or other, cause more anxiety than others.

Even some discussions cause symptoms of stress to appear, to overwhelm. I am talking and suddenly . . . there is a lessening of mental calm, concentration, mood and memory. Always, I must remain vigilant. I must learn to protect myself without submitting to the pressures encountered. Though my heart remains open to the world, I must still avoid certain situations, certain discussions. All this to eventually regain strength and resilience. Rebuilding the self is not an easy nor a swift process.

One step back

As soon as I begin to feel better, I falsely believe everything is "OK." I get the impression I can start living as before again. And then it happens—a step back... Wanting, expecting, striding one large step too big. The fall back is hard. The general anxiety, always hovering at the edge, strikes like a cobra.

I need to size up every situation, to be wary, to be wise to what is possible and what is not. What are those moments that feed my "getting better" and those that suck me dry? I need to manage my mind's thermometer—check every degree of change in temperature if I am ever able to make the right "well-being" choices.

And so, despite the setbacks, it feels good to get out of the house. Focusing on areas to visit that are calm and peaceful. I need those times to gradually re-integrate myself back into a world where re-connection is the goal. After a few forays, testing the waters of the weirdly familiar yet oddly unknown, I discover the wisdom of "step backs"—stepping back rather than pushing forward—not retreating but stepping back to look, to see, to analyze. The art of observation becomes a best tactic, a best friend.

I am at a crossroads. Despite the need to be close to loved ones, I fear the expectations that are part and parcel of socializing. To grow, I need to experience life's pleasures, which outweigh its fears. But to get there, I need to shelve, for now, the mental energies required to give and take. Searching for the right words, the defining words, is difficult. I want to be with, yet apart. My story, everyone else's... They are the same yet different. Our connections... just too complex to decipher at this time. Though I try to verbalize, to explain myself, what I need at this very moment... words cannot convey. And courage is often lacking.

Backing off for a while helps. Eventually, re-beginning a re-integration process becomes possible. But that comes only after making a serious decision to "take care of myself"—both when I am alone and when I am with others—whether it be with family or friends. This means I must rekindle the fires of self-respect rather than self-esteem. Self-esteem is a concept too heavily laden with the expectations of others. Self-respect is from within me and must be my guide.

With time, I begin to look upon things that must get done in a kinder, gentler way—with a less rigid "need" to get them done. I begin to relax the demands I place upon myself and upon everything that surrounds me. A sudden desire to have life enter me as I enter it takes over. By opening the door to spontaneity, I begin to smile again.

Choosing to live well despite this affliction is a seriously positive step. I just can't wait for "the cure." Though this move recognizes the existence of the pain and fears inherent with the "disease"—it nonetheless denies it the power to overtake my every second of every day. Naturally, hitting a few brick walls along the way is par for the course in such an undertaking. You can't want an untrained Doberman as companion without expecting it to nibble if not bite once in a while.

Building confidence

To this environment of healing, I integrate my musical interest in African rhythms. With the arrival of spring, I register for a weekly course in drumming. These classes help build my self-confidence. They also force me to face the complexities of social re-integration. When I feel anger building up deep down inside, rising, boiling up and getting ready to explode, I drum. I drum hard and I drum as loud and powerfully as I can . . . as I want!

Nonetheless, I don't always have the stamina nor the courage to leave my safe haven apartment—to venture out into "getting better." But more often than not when I do, when I can, I come back home feeling energized and most happy that I did put out the required effort to go, to do and to achieve.

Concentration in such situations remains at a premium. An hour's worth expended on a weekly basis takes its toll. I inform the drum teacher of my "health problem." Divulging such a personal "thing" seems to "unlock" me. It seems to free me to be more of me than was before possible.

One evening, I arrive at my drumming classes earlier than usual. We are eight students. After warm-up exercises, the teacher follows up with Tassaba—a West African rhythm common to Guinea. I am into it, but after 20 minutes I suddenly feel a familiar tightening . . . I become anxious—very anxious. The sounds are no longer warm to me. They are rather powerful beats given ominous strength by the group's complete concentration. The collective sound becomes a devastating noise, a nauseous substance. I suddenly need to get out, to get some air. But I freeze—worried, ashamed to abandon my post . . .

On the way home, my mind whirls. I must stop these courses! They are overwhelming me, frightening me again. But as I gradually calm down, I know that I cannot. Doing so would be negative, stepping back too far, admitting defeat, closing the door to progress. And once again I return to the newly acquired mantra: "I will live well, despite."

For some, banal, inconsequential "nothing" things are just that: nothing. For me, though, they can be a serious source of anxious moments and incomprehensible fears rising. Even when I measure the doses of each activity, its pressures, its movements, its consequences in order to assure me a sense of balance, sometimes it isn't enough. What devastates most is that, at times, it takes "nothing" to stoke dormant symptoms that halt my progress.

Breaks

In this up and down, two steps forward, one step back healing process, I discover a need to take several break periods throughout the day. As soon as two hours pass interacting with others, cooking, reading, running errands, I find myself mentally and physically exhausted. A 30-minute break becomes mandatory. At home, this is possible. But I am always afraid of not being able to implement this "break system" in public or social environments. And yet, with planning, it is possible and beneficial. I simply need to respect this need in me and to inform my surroundings in order that this crucial element of my reincarnation is not seen as a personal slight or a form of self-indulgence.

Surprisingly, quiet "away" corners are available anywhere—even if that means using the back seat of a car to lie down for a "pause that refreshes."

Sometimes I feel like a warrior on a spiritual quest. The enemy? Me. I must fight old habits and conditionings. As in fencing, I learn to anticipate the need to step back—lunging only when required. Like a musician, I begin to respect silences in between notes and chords. Knowing when to step forward and be a part of it all again becomes a matter of timing and grace. Everything is an adjustment, readjustment process. What I say and do and how I react, and what others say and do and how they react are more akin to a series of chess moves than aggressive checkers. In essence, coming to an acceptance of this new reality is a must. It boils down to recognizing that, as in all realities, there are limits and limitations.

The perception of experience

I sometimes feel like I am losing my mind, my concentration, my short-term memory and my sense of orientation. All of these seem affected by my illness. But then I see the body as wise and its intelligence, vast. But is it possible to measure intelligence other than in conventional mental or intellectual terms? Is it possible to perceive it in other than rational considerations?

I have come to see my body as having an intelligence of its own. Every time I hear and feel and sense excessive nervousness, palpitations, short breathing, cold sweats, loss of memory and concentration, and rising anger, I see my body speaking, warning of wrongs being highlighted. And with such discoveries, I realize that emotional intelligence is as powerful as any other.

With this illness, intuitions are sharper. Dealings with immediate surroundings more multi-sensorial. Looking at life even seems to require a new set of glasses. Oddly, I begin to see this problem of mine as a sort of privileged sign—one that pushes me to acknowledge a need for better balance in my life, if I am ever to move ahead again. That being the case, new limits are established, and a new direction is calibrated. Though I am still seriously fragile, I start to give this fragility its due, its personal space, its quadrant in my life. And with that, life becomes simpler, clearer, more manageable. Encountering the death and rebirth of a mind is as devastating as encountering it physically. But knowing "it" is life affirming.

Acceptance

The illness

In parenting we are told that being loved unconditionally is the foundation of solid emotional growth for a child. It is no less so when parenting oneself into a new life. We must learn to love our flawed selves unconditionally.

In the challenge that is PTSD, I need to accept myself as I am—a limited, flawed individual, one with an evident fragility and lack of resilience. But this does not mean I must accept myself as a forever defective. But then, what happens if . . . if despite months of therapy and the will to heal there are after-effects? After eight months of sessions, can I actually permit myself to say: "I'm all back. I'm fine!"?

It is a most important day . . . that day when it is possible to stop wishing for a better tomorrow and rather to focus on the wonders and offerings of the present. There are always defined limitations within the walls of a mental health affliction. But there comes a time when it is possible and necessary to allow our souls—"ourselves"— to live fully by accepting life as it is—and that includes accepting the unacceptable as part and parcel of the voyage.

Managing triggers

Crowds

Time slows to a crawl when I enter a crowded area. Though I try to control my breathing, the ensuing dizziness tires me out. My once friendly nature has lost its supple nuances; its welcoming demeanour. My facial features are rigidly fixed, passive, cold and distant. I project the hostility and defiance I feel inside. Laughter echoes in my empty chambers—a joyful sound for and from those around me. I am unable to share or take in any of it. A prisoner of my past, I hurry through such areas, hoping its effects on me will end. It is only when I am no longer surrounded that the tension's stranglehold finally ebbs and subsides.

With each triggering of anxieties, fears, pains, I am forced into a defensive position, into bringing myself back to an acceptable normal. Though I consciously try to avoid such spaces—those environments that trigger the suffering—I am well aware that moving forward demands that I must deal with them, encounter them, confront them. At the onset of such happenings, I have a feeling of crumbling, of needing to fold myself up into an invisible ball. I become anxious. Everyone is perceived as purposefully annoying. And with no evident or logical reason, all I want to do is cry. Often, an incomprehensible need to sleep arises. My mind craves it, my body feels it. But I learn to control this tiredness, this avoidance technique.

To manage the triggers, I try to recognize the self-protective nature of the accompanying emotions. I need their reassurance. Though they are often overwhelming, they are my emotions and I need them to be there for me. If I can successfully associate them with my PTSD it helps me "normalize" or de-dramatize the situation. By rationalizing the link, I tell myself that the reactions are illness related. And when acknowledged, I can then act rather than react and not stay cornered and dysfunctional. To do this (i.e., be able to move forward based on logic) defines the steps taken: massive, though miniature, and progressive, though halting.

To reach such a milestone is noteworthy. It recognizes the effort as worthy, the feasibility obvious, and the tools to do the job of getting out of another morass available. Nothing else could be more encouraging.

Feeling grounded is the best tool for progress. And so, I purposefully walk. Rapid walking connects my body with the earth. When walking, I pay close attention to the environment. It anchors me into a more tangible present: Where am I? What do I see? How do I feel? Who is there? What is there before me, around me?

Walks are usually followed by a short visualization; a reflection and meditation focusing on hope—as in the book: *You Are Here*[11] by Thich Nhat Hanh. I may imagine a flower in need of sustenance, fertilizer, care if it is to grow. An invisible gardener tends to it, tills the earth—and this without even telling me . . . And then I think: How odd, that to grow, a plant needs the decomposed nature of decay to flower as I need my decaying past to nurture the growth of my tomorrows.

Taking charge

A few months after the diagnosis, I continue to question the treatment afforded me. After a year, I decide to take things into my own hands. I want my life back. I want to be in charge again. I do not want to be dependent on others leading me through this mess. In order to get some relief from the residual symptoms of PTSD and to build my stamina, I turn to Chinese medicine. I begin acupuncture treatments not as a replacement for but rather as a complement to the medication and the EMDR therapy.

I seem to react favorably. At first, there is a noticeable improvement that lasts for just a few days after my treatments.

---

[11] Hanh, Thich Nhat, *You Are Here*, Shambhala Publications Inc., Boston, USA, 2009

Eventually, the effects last for a few weeks. I am less anxious. I no longer get the frozen emotions sensation. My sleeping patterns improve. My energy levels rise. And my digestive tract is less constricted. Patterns have changed. I feel more balanced. Encounters are more easily managed as my comfort zone expands. Nonetheless, though life seems to want to continue on its merry way, daily blips reinforce my inability to handle things well. Even simple tasks demand serious consideration. Sometimes, I must reread what I write down. Signing a cheque can take on ominous feelings of anxiety. Some days, I cannot face the ordinary. I must wait for the next day to arrive before going out to do a simple thing such as groceries. Everything is one day at a time and even one step at a time.

When the uneventful or the unexpected causes stress, I lie down comfortably on the sofa or bed to ride it out. It's the law of the pendulum. When stress levels are high, the compensating component must be equal and opposite. And so I rest a lot. And then I exercise some in order to get the balanced feeling back in my head, body and soul.

Joy

Along the lengthy rehabilitation trek, I am enthralled to rediscover what I thought I would never again know: how to feel love and joy. I was so afraid to never feel again, to not be able to overcome the emotional freeze that had overtaken me. I begin giving more and more time to "the present"—to that sense of being in the moment. And with that as a self-directed exercise I begin to perceive life differently. I suddenly view it as immensely beautiful, immensely mysterious and sacred.

Nonetheless, it isn't until the following spring that joy visits me again—and only sporadically ... Desperate to have it "hang about" for a longer period, I try to entice it to stay awhile. I want to nourish it, domesticate it, make it mine again. I try visualization to better prepare a personal space for it. And so I look for sun filled areas, morning, noon and night.

Gradually, in the process of rediscovering it, joy takes on a new dimension. It seems more spiritual than I had ever considered it to be. This new joy seems to demand that I feel it from within rather than from without. In the past I had always expected it from others, from other things and activities, from my marriage, work and social activities. And as much as I continue to enjoy helping and serving others, I now need approval and appreciation less. I want to live more in keeping with my own values and appreciations of others. But for that to be, I also need me to be happy with me.

But even though I may wish to open the door to this precious joy, I still struggle. Sometimes the despair masks my real intent. Sometimes it is the fear or the anxiety that locks joy out.

Nonetheless, I begin to measure the achievements each day brings. This quest for joy pushes me forward. And because I combine my quest with positive action, I see improvements in stress levels. Small steps take on monumental value in strengthening my resolve as I begin to see that achieving inner peace is possible.

A question of shame

To open the door, to open myself up to others, to let even myself in is difficult. Do I do it gradually? Do I have to lay it all out, stranded like a naked beast before the eyes of others? Does vulnerability play a part—possibly turning me into a target? What's the value to all of this? Is it really worth it to lay it all on the line, to say it the way it is? Am I afraid of what "they" will say, how "they" will judge the words coming out of my mouth? Am I fearful of what I myself will discover through this "opening up"?

But then, I tweak the anxiety levels. I need to trust: trust in the capacity of others to be compassionate, trust that just maybe those strangers I fear will become less stranger, less strange. If I make the first move . . . will it give someone discovering my secret a chance to open up also? I need to remember that everyone has baggage— baggage full of personal history, anxieties, insecurities, worries, fears, regrets, challenges and hopes.

Making sense of it all

I am conscious of the fact there are dangers involved in this PTSD scenario. It is so easy to roll up into a ball and to forget it all. It is so easy to just want to be alone, to avoid contact. But then I worry that cutting myself off will make it all worse. What if there is still something worthwhile in me to give, to share? As frightening as it all is, I don't want to give up, to be alone.

And so I try to give ordinary daily tasks a sense of extraordinariness, a value beyond their basic physicality. Doing things like the family laundry, preparing an evening meal, making a list for tomorrow's shopping. These seem petty in the grand scheme of things but I need to make them worthy of being recognized, of having been accomplished, of seeing them as good jobs well done. Why? They transport me beyond myself, beyond my pains and anxieties. And despite the fact they carry much less importance than what I was able to accomplish before . . . they are nonetheless worthy because they open the door to me being with others. They allow in part of the world in which I must gradually relearn to take my place.

Once comfortable with these ordinary things being seen as extraordinary, I begin to believe again that inner peace is possible, that my existence is becoming worthy again.

And so, with the arrival of another winter, I take another step forward—the writing of this book. The getting down to it is encouraging. I do not want to be immobile anymore. Being the prisoner of my own sadness, regrets, sorrows, pains and guilt is too discouraging.

It is obvious that I cannot do anything about my past. But just maybe I can help someone else overcome their horrors. I settle into reading about PTSD, researching it on the Internet—at least as long as my poor concentration can handle it.

In the spring I begin writing in earnest—a few lines a day—and though "slow as it goes," after two years the project is beginning to take shape. I feel it more intensely now. If I can help someone else, it will all have been worthwhile—all of the suffering, all of the fear and regrets and guilt. The writing gives credibility to the hurts but also to the relief. The book holds me up, supports me. It is my survival tool and my chance to flower again. Like a bush whose branches have been crushed, I am suddenly believing that, just maybe, tomorrow is possible.

Opening up

May 2011

Someone is looking at me . . . Ah, it's you. Come to me. I have a secret to share. You are a slave to your secrets but if you set them free they will become your teachers."[12]

A very close friend tells me she has just been diagnosed with a degenerative disease. I am crushed. Faced with this news I realize how vulnerable and useless I feel in light of her plight. I have difficulty focussing, concentrating, speaking, listening. I'm feeling constantly tired, with irregular heartbeats . . . Oddly, I accept to have a drink with you. Yesterday I would have refused. I would have rushed off after having said hello. Staying, accepting is taking a lot out of me, but . . . I feel your warmth, your welcoming manner. And despite the problems I encounter, I take part in our conversation. My secret weighs heavily . . . I'm tired of hiding, of being ashamed. And suddenly, I am comfortable telling you about it—revealing it all. Your compassionate reaction comforts me. I feel at peace.

You open up too, revealing the contents of your own invisible baggage. And suddenly, you are the one seeking compassion. And there we are—both sharing. And by doing so, soaring higher and freer than ever we could have imagined. How wondrous it is to share, to both be emerging from our separate and yet similar cocoons.

---

[12] Hebrew Proverb cited by Ray, J., Adagia hebraica, *Dictionnaire des proverbes, sentences et maximes*, Larousse, Paris, France, 2009

July 25 2011

And yet, despite the soaring and sharing, life goes on. I still face challenges that I have difficulty comprehending.

The psychiatric evaluation

I finally arrive at his office on Sherbrooke Street in Montreal, Quebec. Why am I forced to come here to see him, so far from my home? He is the insurance company's psychiatrist. Despite the fact I left Ottawa early to get here on time, I didn't know there was a Sherbrooke Street East and a Sherbrooke Street West. I am five minutes late. My boyfriend has taken a day off from work to accompany me. He has to. I just cannot drive two hours to Montreal and back alone.

He faces me across the desk. I face him. "Can you explain in your own words," he asks, "what happened at work?" I ask if I can consult my notes. He prefers I not, asking me to simply explain to him in my own words—without notes. I cannot. He stares. I feel judged, intimidated. Two minutes pass—slowly, ever so slowly I find myself unable to say even one word. I am frozen.

"Would it be easier for you to talk about Africa?" he asks. Evidently not. But do I really have a choice?

He stares, waiting patiently for me to speak. Tears fall. I cannot seem to stop crying. I try to share some examples of my experiences in Africa. We have but an hour for me to explain it all. The hour passes by. He asks: "Now, talk to me about your separation from your husband." I add another Kleenex to the pile in front of me. When he finishes doing the rounds—asking about all the stresses in my life, I am no longer able to concentrate. I need help answering his questions. I cannot refer to my notes. But I need them. My memory fails me. When I finally do speak up about a detail, he cuts me off—asking another question.

He explains the difference between a flashback and recall—asking me to tell him which it is that I am speaking about. I tell him: "I think it's a recall, but I'm not sure. Could you re-explain the differences to me?" He curtly answers: "I think my descriptions of them were clear enough."

"With how many men have you lived?" he asks. "How long did you live with each?" "Why didn't these relationships last?" I don't understand what all of these questions have to do with my diagnosis. If only he would allow me to fully answer, to ask even one question.

My pain becomes anger. I feel small and defeated. It takes me a week to get over this meeting.

I stare. He finishes highlighting in yellow in his notepad. Then he writes a few words. Finally, he puts the pen down. This time weighs heavy on my soul for a long time after.

On being judged

August 20, 2011

On this day I learn that—based on an hour and 20 minute meeting with the insurance company's psychiatrist, where I had to travel two hours to get to this meeting to be evaluated, the insurance company demands I return to work within two weeks. I am to return to the same stress-filled environment in which I found it impossible to cope—the same environment that tripped the wires, which revealed my post-traumatic stress disorder. If I do not return to work as ordered, my salary insurance will be cut off.

My doctors had not even been consulted throughout this decision-making process. To this day, I cannot drive by the building where I worked without symptoms manifesting themselves.

Serious bouts of anxiety return and their punch is definitely hard-fisted. I feel like vomiting, screaming, wanting to abandon it all. I can't take it anymore!!! Before the month's end there will be no funds to pay the bills. Through the insurance company psychiatrist, I am deemed a criminal rather than a victim. Though completely dysfunctional, I am ordered back to work. Where do I find the strength to keep on fighting, to overcome the injustice of it all?

I am disillusioned by my own home society. With profits as its catalyst for achievement, it has lost its moral compass, its value system, its humanity.

The injustice

I would so let myself sink slowly into the deep waters I have always embraced . . . let myself be rocked in the bosom of the river until I am no more . . . Defeated and without hope, I hold on by a thread.

I cannot summon the courage nor the strength to work, to cope, to fight. I write for the sole purpose of finding the one ray of hope that I can still hang onto. "Out there," every emotion seems to enter and flow through to stab at my being . . . Thoughts of suicide take hold.

Free fall

August 21, 2011

Destabilized, I am in free fall. I am here and there and everywhere and all at the same time. I grasp at straws, trying to hold on, trying to get my footing. And so I write . . . One moment, I am tired and want to sleep. A split second later, I want to busy myself, my mind, my heart. Agitated, I cannot sleep. Cold as ice and angry, I am distant, impatient, impossible to be with. Totally losing it, I burst into uncontrollable tears every hour.

With a future that has little if anything to offer, I am incapable of calming down, analyzing objectively or finding any solution to my dilemma. Incapable of handling work or anything related to it, I suddenly find myself completely dependent on my companion. With the latest threat regarding finances, I become even more anxious, even more tense and distraught. My relationship and family life are swiftly being negatively affected. An intense anger takes hold of me. How can the insurance company not take into account medical and psychological information that is so easily available to them—information that validates my situation? I can only scream: How immoral!!!

Divine intervention

August 23, 2011

I am cycling. Suddenly I am not alone. A force stronger than any of us is accompanying me—not just now but all along this difficult process. This sudden moment of peace, tranquillity and freedom is overwhelming to the point of stopping me, calming me. I sense it as a miracle happening.

In the past 48 hours of a hurricane-like storm, the waters had become life-threatening. My boat had almost capsized. Today, I find refuge in a small bay where the water is calm and clear. I am no longer seized with fear. I can feel a change, a warm breeze caressing me.

Everything seems straightforward. I know I am on a vast incomprehensible ocean, but I am no longer alone. In a mirage above the waters I am surrounded by a circle of those in need. We hold hands in solidarity. And at the centre of it all a brilliant light that cannot be less than that of the Divine.

August 24, 2011

Despite this episode, this judgmental and final dictate "ordering me to be healthy," I must find the energy, the strength to do for others what I did not receive for myself. No one should have to live through such chaos and turmoil at a time when they can least handle it. I am lucky to not be alone to face and handle such situations. What happens to those who have no one, who are alone to face health issues and loss of financial resources?

I resolve to not let myself be destroyed by this large enterprise. I cannot let it be the reason why I lose it all, lose the progress made. I am well-aware that the erratic emotions I experience are difficult to manage. Compulsive and negative thinking haunts me every night and day; trying to overtake me. Nonetheless, I hang on. Remission is dependent on mental restfulness. It is a must. Even when my body moves, I try to be resourceful by managing the intensity, the energy demanded by every motion; every action. All the while, I tell myself to do what is positive and simple and clean—no frustrating complexities.

In essence: "The challenge in being courageous is to not give up and die but to strive to live."[13]

End of August 2011

I finally choose my battles. I need to fight for me and, in doing so, for those who cannot. I do not have the health to do it on my own, so I ask my family to support me in this quest. I am counseled by my mother who accepts to be my advocate. From her I am able to get the required legal information that will assist me in fighting the insurance company's arbitrary decision.

Communicating with the insurers has become quasi impossible for me. My companion becomes my spokesperson. This is not well-received by the insurance company. They refuse to speak with him. I am the only one they accept to speak "to."

Without hesitation, my doctor and psychologist take on the task of formulating a complaint and request for compensation during this period of difficult transition. Accompanying their strong request are the related medical files as well as the psychological evaluations.

---

[13] Proverb by Vittorio Alfieri, *Oreste* IV, 2

A small miracle

September 2011

A letter arrives. It acknowledges receipt of the submitted medical and psychological files. I am advised that the documents will be reviewed by the insurance company's legal team. I remain without any other communication from the insurance company for two and a half months. The downside: my benefits are immediately cut off.

Will I have enough money on which to survive for the next months? I have no idea. But after only a few weeks, the pressure subsides. In a way, I've already won the battle. I've stopped obsessing about it. And with that, I am more able to focus on what I can do with what I have rather than what I am no longer able to do. And as I look to my partner, I smile and know all is well.

In essence, a reassuring calm has set in. I am neither hopeful nor deflated. I've been able to break free of this 2011 weight on my shoulders.

Out of this hell, grace has flowered. I am off my knees, as it were, beginning to take on whatever happens under my own steam. It seems if anything is to be, I must take the helm of my own ship, and steer madly in the direction I wish to go, and "damn the insurance!" as Admiral David Farragut at the Battle of Mobile Bay, would have assuredly said in my place.

I begin to realize that victory lies in letting go, in accepting what is and how it comes to me. Constantly opposing reality can be seriously damaging. Simply wanting to rekindle inner peace, no more do I ask: *"Why me?"* Through this letting go, I recall Eckhart Tolle's book *The Power of Now*.[14]

---

[14] Eckhart Tolle, *The Power of Now*, Namaste Publishing, Vancouver, Canada, 1999

November 2011

There is a message on my answering machine. I am being asked to call the insurance company as they have reached a decision in my case. Though anxious and untrusting, I gather my courage and return the call. Eventually reaching the one person I must speak to, I am asked: Have you received the retroactive payments of your benefits yet? This total about-face is overwhelming . . . The battle is won!

Year 2012

Breaking out, fighting avoidance

Early January 2012

The gardener (my psychologist) of the emotional and mental garden of my mind makes me aware of things—of things as they are—not as I fear or wish them to be. She tells me that I am doing well . . . Doing better. Though I feel some of that, I also recognize that my life is still filled with way too many avoidance techniques. I have written but three pages in the second chapter of my book—and this because I do not think I can handle the emotions the writing will reveal. And this is not only related to the writing. I continue to avoid certain places, certain people, certain discussions, newspaper articles referring to Africa.

And as all gardeners know well, hoeing, getting to those plants that strangle growth is necessary if a garden is to survive and prosper. She tells me I cannot spend my whole life dependent on crutches. I have to begin holding myself up. Stepping out of my protective bubble is a must, despite the stressful recollections that I will undoubtedly encounter along the way. I need to have confidence in my own progress, in my own growing ability to face head-on life's difficulties. And what I have to recognize is that I now have the tools to move on.

The meeting

January 31, 2012

The first meeting with my counselor, a re-adaptation specialist, is difficult. She has been hired by the insurance company. Though professional and empathetic, I am well-aware her main goal is to facilitate an eventual return to work. And through horrible experience, I have learned not to trust anything that is even remotely related to the insurance company.

But to continue receiving benefits, I must cooperate, allowing for the insurer to play the role they set themselves out to play. And in this case: getting me back to work.

I only agree to meet with the counselor if my psychologist is present.

Despite transparency and congenial exchanges with the insurance company's agent, the objectives being laid out differ. We are advised that after another five months, the insurer will no longer continue paying benefits. Though I remain eligible, the definition of my disability will change as will my access to insurance. It becomes rather clear in the lay down of details that insurance companies are in it for the money and not the well-being of the insured.

Towards the end of the meeting, a reference is made to the psychiatrist I encountered in Montreal. Within seconds, the old symptoms return. I become overwhelmed and anxious. I cannot stop crying.

The counselor leaves the room. It takes nearly 12 hours for me to calm the emotions and fears that so quickly overwhelmed me. My feelings of freedom and progress have disappeared. Once again, I am a prisoner, at the mercy of whatever it is others decide is best for me. I've lost it . . . again . . .

The challenge is great. I am definitely not ready to return to anything that resembles work. Fragile, I once again grab onto my psychological crutches for dear life. With energy ebbing away, I can't understand the logic in these pressures to get me back to work. Is my battery charger defective? Despite all the rest and calming exercises, I can't seem to reach a level of stability or energy storage anymore.

That day reintroduced me to a long and heavy fall into the depths of a darkness I already knew well. The despair was unfathomable and for hours it never left my side. The air was like sand-paper on my skin. Rhythm was no longer a part of my being. Tears fell without end as, into the evening, sadness became despair. Twisted into a nervously twitching ball, I lay on my bed shaking, remembering, reliving what I could not bear to recall of the past few years.

During those moments it was impossible to regain footing. Being, sensing, living in the present was not even a possibility. In the past months, I had learned to centre myself, to recapture stability. Today, I had lost it all again. The feelings were too overwhelming. I was not even here in this room as I tried to regain a foothold. And so, I fell to the floor exhausted.

Unable to focus on the now, I am transported into the past. The shock and the void of fear are so intense I cannot breathe. Time stands still, holding me just below the surface of a raging ocean wave, daring me to rise above the suffocation and pushing me down, ever deeper again.

My partner, as always, is the angel of mercy; so loving, caring, compassionate, giving. He takes out a precious trusted tool: a list of questions recommended by my psychologist for just such moments. He reads the questions aloud one by one. I answer them in writing in a private journal. (See: Chapter 9, Transforming Emotions by Modifying Thoughts.) A half hour later, the emotional intensity ebbs. I fall gently asleep.

Freeing Anxiety

An intense exercise regime, keeps me as grounded as I can hope to be. After a full session, I feel physically and mentally rejuvenated. In winter, I strike out on long stretches of cross-country skiing.

During the month of February, I write. Then I ski some more... Despite storms on the horizon, I head out, face it, dare it to snow. Through every tiny step, I feel stronger, more powerful, more belligerent.

The attack

March 21, 2012

It is a wondrously beautiful spring day. For the first time, I can cycle rather than ski. It is 20 degrees Celsius. I am thrilled at the prospect of wind in my face. The sun melts the last vestiges of snow. I hear birds signing and water gurgling in the now fast running creek bed.

I feel great—fulfilled and happy. I can see a light at the end of my dark and heavy tunnel. Things are looking up. Everything is quiet—few if any cars. Everyone at this hour is away at work. I follow the river along our curving road, feeling the warm sun on my face. I smile.

I wave hello to a neighbour. She is outdoors with her children. I notice her two dogs. After a 45-minute ride, I head back home. I am about two kilometers from a brisk cup of tea. The neighbour is still outdoors with the children. As I pass by, I feel a heaviness against my leg, an instant yet silent pain. My thigh is bloody. One of the dogs has attacked. I stop riding. I scream. The dog runs around the bicycle and bites my other thigh. Frightened, angered, I become livid!

I ride on as best I can; crying, angry, afraid now. My biking shorts are shredded. I am bleeding. Enraged by the attack, I scream at the neighbour. She retreats, apologizing for having to go—to care for her young son. And so, I am alone . . . No one is on the road to help in any way. I pedal with difficulty, hoping my partner will be home.

He sees me in pain and accompanies me to our room. As he tends to my wounds, I lie dazed, in shock. Michael calls the police. My heart beats uncontrollably, my throat dry. And I feel it coming on, a fragility, a deep fear and worry settling in despite my trying to stay calm.

The police arrive. I am questioned. A report is filed. I must go to the clinic. Even though I have already been vaccinated, I require another shot to ward off a potential rabies infection.

For several days I lie in bed, waiting for the wounds to close, to heal. For several weeks, sitting is uncomfortable. Night time is worse. A plague of nightmares erupts, disturbing my every sleeping hour. Sweat runs down my chest, soaking the bed.

The next three weeks are a challenge. My nervous system had become calmer, more resilient. Now, I am back to square one. Anxious, my feelings of security and comfort have all but vanished. I am once again a victim. I am now afraid to leave the house for a walk. I fear another attack. Dogs, in our country neighbourhood, are often not restrained. They own the neighbourhood.

Another week goes by. I am now increasingly determined to not be cowed by this event. I need to regain control, or I won't ever get it back. I carry pepper spray, especially designed for protection against aggressive dogs. On a first outing, I am accompanied by my partner. The next day we are out again. Then . . . I try it alone. My heart beats wildly as my whole body trembles. But I know I must do it if I am ever to again feel safe on my own. Gradually, after a few more days, I am able to walk by the spot . . . The same spot where I was attacked.

Nonetheless, despite all the efforts to desensitize myself from this event, I still cannot use my bicycle. I am still too afraid. When I hear a dog bark, I freeze. Nonetheless, I am determined. To compensate, I carry my dog-spray and continue to do my walks and runs.

Choosing a voice

I try to make sense of things that happen to me. This is the second time I am attacked by a dog. How odd that is. And yet, I continue to believe that there is a reason for everything—even though sometimes what occurs makes no sense. Nothing happens for nothing. Following this shock to my system, I register for three reflexology treatments. Since I have already been considering taking up this specialty for myself, I wondered what effect a series of treatments would have subsequent to my traumatic event.

Through the application of hands at various pressure point areas in the feet, face and ears, glands and organs become stimulated. Due to my experience with the dogs and the subsequent emotional consequences, the focus of these treatments is on specific reflex points related to the nervous system.

I am thrilled with the feelings of well-being realized through these sessions. After every treatment, I feel more and more grounded, more and more calm. My sleep patterns improve. Constantly being on edge subsides. With those results, I am resolved. This is definitely the field I wish to enter. As I have always enjoyed giving foot massages and now knowing the true benefits to those in need, I am convinced my choice is the right one.

End of March, I begin training part-time in reflexology. It is a three-month course. I can handle one morning a week. My concentration is improving, but one day a week, for three hours, is all I can handle. Even then, after the training sessions, I am exhausted for the next two days. Yet, despite this slow progress I feel invigorated. And so, one day at a time, I move ahead once again.

Stabilizing the wound

July, 2012

It's been two years since my diagnosis. One and a half years of desensitization sessions and a whole lot of effort in the hope of finally, one day feeling OK.

I see myself as much more functional than I once was in social and family situations. I go out. I socialize some. I study. I live . . . I live with a healing wound. I accept that I am no longer who I was "before." In a sense, I see myself as having surpassed the expectations of that past life. Nonetheless, I am still vulnerable. My intellectual capacities have been sorely tested. My ability to handle stress also.

Schedules remain rigidly managed. There must always be a time for rest in between each activity. Pauses are required throughout the day. Different times in the year, especially specific dates, are more difficult to handle. The body seems to have memorized the shock and pain of events. It becomes increasingly important for me to deal with this by gauging the required responses to the pains. Though I push myself to become more and more a part of life as it is lived with and by others, I continue, at this moment in time, to measure what is possible and what is not. In essence, I respect the power of weak moments as it affects my ability to handle them. By doing so, I offer myself a better opportunity to both understand and overcome the related anxieties assailing me.

The apprenticeship

August, 2012

With progress showing itself to be more and more stable, I push harder, try more and accomplish more. But when I push too hard, try too much, I risk falling . . . It is always a question of balance. I must always calculate the amount of energy required to do anything.

Before I am eligible to complete my reflexology exam, 60 apprenticeship treatments are required. These will test both my knowledge and capacity to succeed at this venture. I am responsible for scheduling all the sessions and establishing a rhythm based on my personal strengths. Throughout all of this, I also must curb my perfectionist tendencies; my consistently demanding personal expectations.

All in all, I don't find the process easy. The world moves at a much faster pace than mine; follows a much quicker rhythm than I do now. The minute I step outside my own space, I see it all roll by at such a mesmerizing speed. People, technology, society in general; everyone is running while I can only walk. To be able to stand solidly on my own, I need a slower, more determined, more stable pacing. And that means not expecting to achieve the same results or as quickly as someone else. Process becomes king. Quality over speed is paramount as the end product, though of quality, becomes secondary.

Questions, always questions must be asked. Have I respected my limits today? Have I overdone things; rendering me uncomfortable or insecure? What of my energy? Am I overtaxing it? Am I taking care of myself in order to maintain a healthy balance? Do I have a smile on my face? If not, why not? How do I keep myself from falling back into negative habits? Is the questioning of myself enough? Are ruminations about my habits enough? Or should I rely more on a psychological review of where I am at, at this particular moment in time?

Overall, I discover that by ignoring what others think, demand or want from me is liberating. When I feel at my best, it is like having wings. I am free. I discover that the physical, mental, and spiritual space I inhabit must first and foremost be mine, no one else's. That way, I can expand outward and toward others from a solid foundation of self-respect.

Work

Autumn 2012

It is a big day. I am returning to work. It is part time. I'll be giving two reflexology treatments a week. I feel good in this work environment. It allows me the freedom to establish a work rhythm that meets the needs of my health concerns. That I can rest between sessions is more than a plus. It is required if I am ever to make a success of this return to the work world.

Slowly I adapt myself to this new quest. Everything is a discovery, a new challenge. I am both building a client base and confirming to myself what my abilities and capacities are. Post-treatment comments from clients are positive. I am encouraged. A new feeling arises . . . A sense of accomplishment. Though only the beginning, it is a successful step forward. I know that none of this would have been possible two years ago.

Rebirth

The homeless man

As I head to my car after this wonderful day, I see you there . . . Your arm stretches out; the cup awaiting a dollar, 25 cents, anything. Sitting on the sidewalk, hair dishevelled, frozen fingers, filthy coat, you seek some fragment of warmth from the sun, from us all.

I see myself in your eyes. Without family? Lost, alcoholic, drug-dependent? A forgotten veteran? If I had not had family support and encouragement, good mentors, and the right tools to rise from my sidewalk . . . Where would I be?

You can't work. You've been floored by your traumas. But you've found your solace through drinking, smoking, sniffing, injecting. And though you've chased your demons away, the damned things keep coming back. They haunt you; day after day, night after night. Your watery eyes, their vision blurred by misery reminds me of the gifts that are mine; how lucky I am. I had choices. Did you? I was encouraged. Were you? I was given the tools to survive. You weren't . . .

I was given choices, a chance to survive. And so, tonight, I cry the deepest of cries for you.

Year 2013

Energy

The past seems to now have a lesser hold on me. New dreams are taking hold; taking root. What once limited my outlook is morphing into potential. What appears to be a better tomorrow is founded on more positive perceptions, actions and a gradual realignment of my compass. Its needle for the most part now points north, outlining more clearly a way forward. And though at times it may have a propensity to veer southward, a better knowledge of my physical, mental and emotional requirements, a clearer thinking and determination all combine to bring me back on course.

At first, I seemed to lack the physical energy to move forward. I lacked the resilience to take on positive steps. But, gradually, a change occurred. And this change was rooted in my energy levels.

In the spring of 2012, an acupuncturist recommended I undertake a hypotoxic diet to increase those levels. For more than a year I hesitated. Why would I deprive myself of all the pleasurable tastes available to me in cheeses, desserts, pasta, etc.?

But in the spring of 2013, I finally commit by adopting most of the recommendations of Jacqueline Lagacé.[15] Refined sugars, milk products and gluten are gradually eliminated from my diet. In essence, the goal is to understand and mediate the effects modern eating habits and contemporary food configurations have on our digestive systems. By gradually educating myself on the topic, it becomes easier to submit to the changes required in daily food preparation and eating habits. Over the next few months, I notice a change. I am more energized. Where a once entrenched fatigue weighed heavy on my shoulders, I now feel lighter.

---

[15] Lagacé, Jacqueline, PhD, *The End of Pain: How Nutrition and Diet Can Fight Chronic Inflammatory Disease*, Greystone Books Ltd., USA, 2014

Nonetheless, dinner dates at friends' or restaurant invitations are not refused. I accept as usual, savoring every mouthful available on the menu. Becoming a purist is not in the cards for me. As always, health is a matter of balance.

Potential

In June of 2013, I begin a three-day training program on the principles of coaching and integral development. It is the first time I find myself in a position of having to introduce myself to a group—and to speak of the paths taken that have brought me to "now." It is a rather destabilizing moment . . . But once the ice is broken, I begin sailing on a vast sea of discovery and learning where before me lies an endless horizon of limitless possibilities.

And so, it is with this widening perception of horizons that I find myself once again able to dream; able to allow my imagination to soar.

For three years, I saw myself as having lost resilience. Stress had taken over. My body was convinced of it. My habits confirmed these perceptions. But what if? What if I could see the possibility of living otherwise? What if I could see myself open to revising these perceptions; to believing otherwise? What if my limitations could be redefined as potential?

I am reminded that there are those on this earth whose very existence is rooted in inspiration. Nelson Mandela, after years of incarceration, succeeded in overcoming the inherent limitations and restrictions of his prison environment. Rather than submit to baser emotions and feelings, he chose to fight, to elevate himself above them individually and collectively. As he nurtured the power of his intentions, they grew stronger than the subjugation that for years he was made to endure. And because of this intent, this determination, Mandela overcame everything imposed upon him: be it fear, sadness, anxiety, anger—all elements that, individually or combined, could have caused total disintegration of the self. And from this determination arose an inspiring quest to create, to gently "inflict" justice upon the world.

Reality, whatever it be, repeats itself for the simple reason that we don't change our thinking or the conditions that maintain the status quo. If we wish for change, if we wish to know happiness rather than sadness, freedom rather than guilt, courage over fear, health over sickness, believing in the possible is what brings about the required potential to alter any reality. Mandela showed the way.

Is coping with, dealing with, handling and overcoming illness possible through a better understanding of what the mind can do? A workshop with Dr. Joe Dispenza[16] of Connecticut helped me to change my perceptions. Through his teachings I began to see my limitations and the value of my increasing knowledge in a different light.

During stressful periods, the brain, fragmented by instability, functions erratically. Our thoughts create a chemical reaction that forms both a closed resistive-to-change circuit and trains the body to react accordingly. And when that stress is powerful enough to limit our ability to think otherwise, we become dependent on a cancerous emotional response. Basically, we come to memorize neurochemical responses and they, in turn, begin to define or redefine our personality. Determination and perseverance are required to alter this neurologically closed circuit. It is like radically modifying the operating system of a resistant computer—not easy but essential.

By repeating over and over; by integrating and assimilating an altered stance, a transformation begins to occur not only in our neurological responses but also in our chemical and genetic or causal antecedents.

And with this cleansing of the neurological environment, the brain is given the opportunity to recalibrate—to re-become coherent.

---

[16] Dispenza, Dr. Joe, *Breaking the Habit of Being Yourself*, Hay House, Inc., Carlsbad, USA, 2012

In that quest, meditation has been a key element that has allowed my subconscious to soothe, to tone down the analytical brain and, through this process, to re-energize my ability to take on a new, more vital reality.

I chose to integrate this conditioning process into my life for the simple reason that it works for me. It arms me with the tools required to face down and deal with those times when I feel vulnerable; those times when past traumas seek to overwhelm me. And when I compare my 2010 capacities in the area of survival to those of today, it is evident that my conscious determination along with a concomitant meditation practice have shown themselves to have been crucial to the progress achieved. For in the end, there is no more encouraging, nor a more revitalizing gift we can offer ourselves than to "take back" what is intrinsically ours: the ability to control our own lives.

Chapter 6: Rebuilding my Life

Despite the daily struggles required to rebuild the infrastructure of my life, I was beginning to feel like I still had choices and a deep abiding faith that dictated that one day all would be well. I chose to believe that healing, in whatever circumstance, was possible... nevertheless. I chose to never abandon that belief, even when things were at their most horrendous. And because of this, I simply didn't feel alone—even at the worst of times. I "know" there is a divine presence accompanying me at all times. Otherwise...

Nonetheless, for the longest time I was so so angry. There was so much to take in, to leave behind; to understand and to reject. And now, I need to forgive myself and to forgive others; to acknowledge and to set aside both the aches I created and those hurting me from within and without. And throughout this reconstruction, this renovation, this rejuvenation, I recognize a very important facet of this progress: I recognize those who, despite it all, are still here, accompanying me. And with that, I discover the importance of those who have abandoned me and those who, for all intents and purposes, must be left behind.

Meditation and Prayer

In order to overcome, understand, weigh and analyze all that's happening, I find that I must go beyond myself. And so, I have begun researching, reading on and discovering the words of wisdom to be found in spiritual, philosophical and religious readings. Through this daily exercise in discovery, I am searching for the sacred fire of my being—my sacred fire; the light leading me forward.

Rebuilding oneself is extremely difficult at first. The gentle mood-altering capacity of meditation is not exactly in the cards when chaos is all we see in the mirror. Feeling lost, disconnected, anxious. These are not the stimulants we need to achieve inner peace. And so, I depend on the hope of a better tomorrow.

Today, I light a candle. I am in a quiet place. All I hear is silence, a calm reflection of my desire to move forward. Sitting comfortably, wrapped in a warm blanket, I listen to myself breathe, like a bird on a swaying branch.

I take in two deep breaths, in and out slowly. I repeat this again. Gradually, the breathing feels more and more natural, comfortable. A thought comes forward, I observe it, let it go. As I sit calmly breathing I become that breath, feeling the air slip in and out through extended nostrils; going into and leaving my body. After a while I am more and more present in both time and space. An odd feeling of ease and gentleness allows my thoughts to become "unlost," un-puzzled, uncomplicated. I feel lighter, and then even more light. A weight lifts. My soul relaxes as I listen to myself becoming better.

Exercise

I am running today; running contentedly. The more I am comfortable in my own skin, the more I feel alive. I find pleasure in "living within me." My breathing is becoming powerful yet calm. Discovering the peace to be found in nature is a balm on my aches and scarred wounds. Though I need to breathe in the society around me, I need an environment that does not always demand my presence nor my participation; I need to simply be free within it. And it is in full forests that I have found that freedom. Birds, scattering squirrels and chipmunks, the fluttering of leaves and the trickle sounds of creek water. In such places, where freedom and I convene, I discover breezes that are not shy to caress my face; urging me forward, pushing me further as I expend energy and gather even more into me with each silently pounding step of my runners.

Yesterday my legs felt heavy, my spirits low. I was weakened by whatever; tired for some reason or other. The effort required to get out from under, to step outside and breathe-in deeply was difficult. I needed discipline to intervene in my procrastination.

The days following my therapy sessions were always difficult. The EMDR process jumbles the rigid mess of our insides as it makes room for progress. Visions of that which must not be revisited reappear. Stifled emotions that need to be even more stifled act up . . .

Running liberates. Cardio isn't just cardio. It takes the pain away, as my body stabs through the air and my heart screams under my breath. And then gradually, with the last of fiery breaths exhaled, calm reasserts itself. If it was not for the running, would my family life have survived?

And so, summers bring diving into a river's exhilarating waters, and winters the thrusting glides of rhythmic skis on trails to nowhere. The movement, the effort, the muscle aches make the red hot embers of anger go away, calm the anxieties and bring on increasing feelings of freedom and well-being.

Holistic approach

Every activity I take on has a specific goal in mind: and that is to bind and stabilize the wounds I have encountered. In the quest to rediscover the me that is there—what is left of what I was—which now molds the shape of what I am becoming, I need new points of reference. I need a disciplined daily routine. I need to relearn how to trust myself and to trust in life.

During the first year of rehabilitation, I focus on structure, on thrusting forward through physical activities and a disciplined routine. These calm the stresses, the anxieties and the ever-invasive disruptive emotions. And this is what I consider to be my holistic approach. Simple as it is, it takes into account all of the dimensions of my being in need of reconstruction: my heart, my mind, my body, my soul.

Music

My piano

Everyone has personal interests that are unique to their being. Whether it is mechanics, flower arranging or dancing, is irrelevant. Personal interests define who we are through what we do. I am moved by music.

Music is my refuge. My soul is uplifted when I hear, compose or play music. The words I write, the sounds I create resonate throughout our home. All the notes filling the air are for me the most natural scents and sensual concoctions of nature's most exquisite perfumes.

I write ... notes, words, chapters, songs. Fifteen minutes, 30 minutes, an hour, two hours ... Gently, progressively more and progressively freer ...

As with anyone else in "this" situation, there is a need to free everything that is bottled up, menacing, discouraging and destructive. Survival depends on it. However we achieve this is how we achieve it. In my case, the piano is there to listen to my soul sounds, to absorb through my fingers the suffering and the loneliness ... and to liberate me from them.

In music, I am off on a wondrous trip without need for a map. Every road is delicious. I raise myself up to the skies and walk "scrunchily" through the snow and beach sands of rolling dunes. I cross tumultuous oceans only to reach the other side's gentle waves lapping at a child's tickled toes. In essence, it is necessary to lose oneself through a soul search in order to solidly, realistically and positively rediscover both ourselves and our way back to ourselves.

Percussion

Sometimes, words are not enough to say what needs saying. Sometimes, re-establishing natural rhythms requires cadence, intense emotions require channelling, and anger requires loosening up. In those moments I take out the *djembé* (African drum). I close the windows and begin drumming and drumming and drumming until sweat streams from my brow and anger and fear from my spirit ...

Art Therapy

The other day, I was in very troubled waters. The waves within me were monstrous and dangerous. The disc in my head was spinning wildly, endlessly repeating all the visions of injustice I had encountered during my African foray.

I took out the book *Le journal créatif*[17] by Anne-Marie Jobin. I consulted the index.

What to do when seriously angry

To add an environment for my feelings, I add heavy metal to the background. I raise the volume uberhigh. I grab some coloured pencils and large sheets of paper. Is red available??? I'm going to need it!

The sheets are soon covered in the angriest strokes of intense colour ever. I have created them, and now I hide them. They are too private, too angry, too ugly. But today, ugly is good. I stop the music and begin writing in my journal; three pages, without thinking, rapidly. Each sentence begins with: I feel. . .

After an hour, I am calm again . . . I can restart the day.

Tonight I probably will have a bad night—a night of nightmares. The morning will be difficult.

I probably will be losing it again, but I will, eventually, move north of darkness—if only with my pile of coloured pencils, sheets of paper and Anne-Marie Jobin's book *Le journal créatif.* Through her book, she invites me to explore dreams, both my shallows and my depths. Through various exercises, using writing and drawing, I do not achieve artistic greatness but getting to the bottom of things becomes easier. Hers is a world of encouragement, of self-fulfilment of discovery of inner truths.

Rest

If I spend most of my mornings weeding my interior garden-scape

---

[17] Jobin, Anne-Marie, *Le Journal Créatif*, Éditions du Roseau, Montréal, Canada, 2002

through various creative techniques, I prioritize my afternoons for rest. Every day, I nap for at least one hour.

Sometimes I question the validity of that discipline. Is this "nap thing" an avoidance of reality technique, a symptom of depressive thinking or am I legitimately tired? Not knowing may be a good thing as I try ever harder to increase my capacities to handle more and more every day.

Nonetheless, I learn that sleep is a good thing. It relates to physical, emotional and mental issues. Not wanting to miss out on a good thing, I also go to bed early every day. An increased sense of humour and calm is the result. I also do not hesitate to take sleeping medication, if need be. To this day, I continue taking naps. They are crucial to my well-being.

Humour

During the last two years, often too tired to do anything else, I've watched a lot of television and listened to a lot of music. I nonetheless choose wisely. To keep things on the "up and up" I chose comedy over everything else. If I cannot find a movie worth watching, I head to the comedy section of YouTube. I get a royal kick out of Russell Peters.

Though my soul is not yet comfortable with laughter . . . I do find myself giggling once in a while.

Alcohol

Though at times I'd like nothing better than to get three sheets to the wind, I generally avoid alcohol. It has a tendency to aggravate depression and goes against the goals I have set for myself. I prefer being surrounded with positive and loving people, a calm environment and healthy foods. Basically, I focus on doing what is required to feed my soul and going where it is possible to achieve this goal.

It is only since 2012; since I completed my desensitization treatments, that I have been able to, occasionally, have a glass or two—and this without feeling too much under the weather the next day.

In the end, it is always a personal choice. So it has been best for me to focus on other venues, other more positive ways, to alleviate the sometimes too full glass of emotions that I may encounter. Naturally, the temptation is always there—the temptation to flee; to run rather than to stand firm. But then, since none of us are perfect, there are times when we lose our footing; when we forget everything we have learned. All that to say: every day is a new day. Every day we know the trek must be restarted from step one. The questions are always the same: What choices will I face today? What choices will I make to handle situations; to handle "me"?

Therapeutic Massage

Monthly, I allow myself the calming effects of a professional therapeutic massage. It lowers anxiety and physical tension levels.

Yoga

It is a given that anything that provides relaxation, calm and spiritual harmony is a worthy exercise.

Yoga is very much a tension reliever. It encourages spiritual and physical flexibility. Respiration, which is often affected by anxiety, deepens and is enriched through yoga. And as breathing is often defined as the interface between the spiritual and the physical, I try to find more and better ways to inhabit my body, to render it more and better grounded.

Visualization

The Tree

Following my yoga exercises, I sit comfortably, back straight, eyes closed, feet firmly planted. I concentrate on my breathing—each inhale and exhale of air. This 10-minute session is focused on anchoring, rooting myself to the earth; "seeing" my body receiving all the required nutrients from it.

Affirmations

Despite stumbling now and then, I observe and analyze my thoughts. The goal is to free myself of negativity. I stand before a mirror reciting self-composed affirmations[18] to help rebuild my confidence. The goal again? Bid adieu to what is harmful to me.

I find the acts of visualizing and affirming to be powerful exercises. They not only alleviate the negative but promote a forward-moving reprogramming process. They tend to counter-balance taking ourselves too seriously; a consideration that our every thoughts are truth when in fact they may be nothing more than vague perceptions of what is. Reality inevitably incorporates elements of our personal thoughts, but in reality (no pun intended) it encompasses much more than one person's analysis of it.

Light

I finish my day as I start it. Either by lying or sitting on the bed, I imagine my heart as a sun. Its rays are warm and comforting. I visualize its light entering each of my limbs, eventually encompassing the whole of my being. I then see that light exit me... now surrounding me. I calmly inhale and exhale while imagining this source of energy as love.

Through my own experience I have discovered that every human being has a certain capacity to self-heal, to choose what we would wish our interior state to be, and to determine what our thoughts can and should be. And through such notions, it then becomes possible through visualizations and meditation to cultivate and nurture a luminous state of wellness.

---

[18] Hay, Louise L., *You Can Heal Your Life*, Hay House, Inc., Carlsbad, USA, 2004

Giving to others

Through this reconstructive process, this taking-charge, a crucial element arises: the very idea of "others." How do we maintain a healthy contact with others when we feel so weak and vulnerable, angry, and at times desperate? How do we rise above victimhood and self-pity?

Every day I try to email someone, make a phone call—do something to maintain contact. When I isolate myself too much, I begin to stagnate, to lose my way again. Even when it is difficult, I strive to be available, to be useful to others—especially my family. Whatever the intent, it is always good to reach out, to get out of my protective shell.

In the end, what is important is not the scope of an action but rather the very fact of the action itself. Yesterday, I wrote two love notes—one to my husband, one to my step-daughter. Three short lines, nothing more. The day before, I washed and folded their clothes. If for so long living had become a daily struggle, I can only imagine the patience and effort that has been required of them in the trying to understand and in the adaption to my illness. They were and remain the ones who are owed a medal of survival!

Chapter 7: A Support Network

Autumn 2010

Human contact is difficult. Every minuscule effort to "function" tires me out. To discuss anything with any semblance of logic is a tremendous challenge. I cannot spend more than an hour "trying" that I do not need a place to lay down and rest. My resilience, my capacity to face anything is so low I cannot control my frequent blow-ups.

I can see and feel my parents worry during the rare visits I pay them. Though I can hide some of my symptoms, I can't avoid the "looks." Where there was once evident, lively repartee my face is rigidly frozen, my eyes lifeless. Emotionally and psychologically I am no longer present.

Months pass . . . I begin to accept what has become of me. And with that recognition, I gradually open myself up to what it is that is gnawing at my soul. With a dogged determination I delve into the "what" of what is happening. Slowly, it becomes increasingly possible to reach out, to try to explain. And with this door of knowledge opening wider, my communications become less cutting, less icy; relationships regain their warm footings. My family becomes more a part of the move forward and less the audience to an uncontrollable drama. Though progress is slow, everyone, including me, is encouraged. We all begin to believe that a better tomorrow is possible.

And with that, I am more able to stretch beyond what is, to try even harder to overcome what is eating at me.

My biggest challenge is the "alone times." Despite family and friends being there for me, I feel disconnected. No one can understand what I am living deep down inside of me. And because this is so, the loneliness is often unbearable.

Through my family and a friend's connections, I make the acquaintance of two people who have gone through rough times due to PTSD. They become my peer group. The connectedness we share is comforting. And though we meet only sporadically, those encounters lead me out and away from isolation.

Over and above new connections, I share with my best friend the pains I encounter. Despite the geographic distance between us, and possibly because we are now partnered in each our own struggles, one physical, one mental, we are ever closer. She is a woman worthy of the utmost admiration. Despite her own battles, she gives to me. She encourages, motivates and is nothing less than a beacon of hope. For the past 28 years we have shared emotions and experiences together. And always my words, happiness and sadness found respite in the bosom of her soul.

During the first months of my illness, my actions and reactions were mechanical, wooden, robotic—my soul frozen, rigid. By opening up, family connections became more harmonious. I now try to better identify and explain my symptoms and needs by saying them outright: "I need a huge hug right now." This is a massive step forward as through clarity others more easily relate to what they do not understand. It also stops people from feeling as if they have to gingerly walk on eggshells around me. Mental health issues are not given to being understood, and because this is so, no one knows how to react, what to say or how to say it. In the end, it is up to me to reassure those around me that "It's OK"—I won't crumble. "You're not responsible for me being sad, being upset, being impatient. It's part of the shit I'm going through." And so, when good intentions and actions or words do not help, I say so.

In the end, the most comforting gifts are those of affection and listening.

A primary need for me is to maintain and nourish my relationships with family and friends. Even if it is a five-minute call, an email or a short visit. I am calmed and encouraged by verbalizing and manifesting my gratitude and love. My family needs this recognition. It is difficult for them to see me going through all of this. For all intents and purposes, I must also encourage my family to "get beyond it all"—to go out and enjoy life; my problems should not stop them from being what I need them to be—happy and themselves.

In the beginning, progress is slow. It seems to require privatization—as if it is mine alone to take in and deal with. Each step taken requires that I be reassured that it actually is a step forward. I therefore divulge progress in small doses. In essence, I am at a stage where sharing the deepest of thoughts and feelings is only possible with my therapist. It is only gradually that I am able to finally bring more people into my hard to understand world.

What a blessing it is to have a partner who sees this episode in our lives as a growing experience, a time to hone his skills in the areas of patience and compassion.

To love and allow oneself to be loved

When you look at me, do you see the woman I am or the illness?

I assert my capacities, my limits and this to manage my symptoms. I am completely invested in my recovery. I am presently incapable of following your rhythms, your pace. I am just beginning to appreciate my own. I don't even see it anymore as a handicap but rather as a gift—one that permits me to once again love myself, to respect myself as is. I want to loudly proclaim this renewed caring from the top of a mountain—the very one I climbed to finally achieve this recognition of "me" as worthy.

My heart goes out to you and is sad at the same time. I can't even promise you a better tomorrow. Though I am beginning to accept my limitations, my difference, I need to continue on this journey of rediscovery without promises or a look beyond. Contentment is as far as I can stretch. It is like a soft textured bandage on my wound. Through all of this, can you still see me as worthy?

Descended from the heights of that goal-laden mountain, the world is a vast sea before me, and my heart a wave drenched beach. You are there. You take my hand gently. You accept what is. You understand that I am no longer the woman you once knew and sadly grieve the loss. Before us lies a patch quilt of the past, present and future. The past to which you had given yourself totally, during which you accompanied me without reservation—despite its pain and suffering and during which you also put aside some of your own needs. The present, the now, this light-filled environment that glows from our discoveries, our acceptance of what is, our love strengthened and evolving. And the future? Do you see the rainbow?

My role models

On those days when I cannot cope, when I am at the end of my rope, I think of one person who was able to overcome all difficulties despite the odds. My mother is that woman. She is strong, positive, resilient. Never once has she allowed herself to be beaten by the oh so numerous challenges that over time have presented themselves to her. To this day, she continues to face life head-on. Without preconceived notions of self-aggrandizement, she has the wisdom to ask the right people for help and guidance from those who generously have it to give. Above all, she is an incomparable model of strength and generosity. To her, whatever I choose to do and whatever happens to me, I must always take the needs of others into consideration. And from her I have received the greatest gifts: to be strong despite anything, to be generous and to be sensitive.

My adoptive father, first and foremost, gave me his greatest gift. He loved me. He chose me. He has been and continues to be a huge gift to my life. He has given me permission to give myself permission to believe that everything is possible; that my words and music are worthy of being read and listened to. He has always given me wings and encouraged my creativity. He is frank and direct and never despairs, despite the challenges before me. "It is not what happens to you but what you do with what happens to you that counts." His heart beats to the same rhythm as my mother's. There's is an incomparable determination founded on rich human values carved in an undeniable and always constant consideration for others.

I have been blessed . . .

A reason for being

The child

In your eyes I see light and love, which calm the torrent of emotions assailing me. You are the sun whose rays transform pain. Your tenderness is a salve to my illness. Through your laughter, the weight I carry is that much less.

I am blessed by your presence. You give me a reason for being.

Today, I must leave the house—pick you up from daycare. Actually, you depend on me more and more as your father is busy building our new home. I pray that I never disappoint you. Though I don't always have a smile that actually smiles, I do try to be there for you.

I would hope that I am a worthy guide for you. I do so wish for you a luminous future, one in which it is normal and good to be understanding and sensitive towards others. I do so pray that you would understand and appreciate difference, empathize with those who are handicapped; and care for those who may be ill.

I am there for you and always will be. My love for you is unconditional. You are the daughter of your mother and father. I am the stepmother—if that is acceptable to you. Am I worthy of your love that is so great and pure? In response I would simply hope that I am and ask that you accept mine.

Despite the fact you are already extraordinary just as you are, I hope that this trial and tribulation time that we are experiencing together as a family will add to that extraordinariness—making you an even deeper, wiser and more compassionate person.

In that wondrous face of yours, I see a fire that helps keep my heart's embers burning. You enliven the child in me. The world becomes unbelievable when I see it through your eyes—more lively, more imaginative and light. You are a gift that transforms my life with each encounter.

Thank you Orlane.

The Divine

I weigh the heft of the words that define this wonderful day. My lover is looking at me with intense joy, with an almost impossible love. Endless tears fall, streaming over my features.

On this Easter day 2011, I have renewed my faith in the greatness of "You" God; a faith that has been sorely tested since my departure for Africa. Your light manifests itself brilliantly through this divine energy that seems to glow between he and I. Silence rings us, brings us warmly together.

I have fallen profoundly in love with this soulmate at my side. So many qualities discovered and continuously reverberating in this man: patience, generosity, presence, sensitivity, compassion . . .

Our passionate love has become true love. We have become two souls interlocked in a quest of ever growing respect and love. We seek to bring about the best in each other. Despite a turbulent ocean-crossing, the ship still sails. Despite my illness, we have become stronger, more unified in our visions for tomorrow. Oddly, this illness has served as a catalyst for love.

I hear Your gentle voice speaking to me of love, of forgiveness, of joy and peace. I have resisted love for so long. I have feared it; feared not being able to give it, get it, share it. Today, I give in to it; to Your divine love in him and Your divine love in me. I choose to be loved. I choose You, Lord, blessing me, and because of this I choose him to love me and me to love him.

"My love, I want to marry." *Tears stream down his face and meld with mine.*

Chapter 8: The Future: Being Free, Reborn

On one hand illness, and more specifically post-traumatic stress disorder, can lead to a disassociation of body and spirit and the sentiment that we are a stranger to both others and to ourselves.

From another perspective, healing introduces "re-connection," rediscovering the existence of self beyond the life we had before. It is a chance to travel to a depth unknown to us previously—to find a new self, our new self—better than the one that existed before. Possibly, it is a re-alignment within the realm of our true nature, which allows for that re-connection with ourselves and others to be.

The numerous losses—that of my former husband, my job, my reputation, my health . . . All of these gave me pause and a choice. The choice . . . once it was actually possible, was obvious: growth. Through the loss of ego and my social identity, I discovered the possibility of rebuilding "differently"—on a more solid footing: on one based on my own set of values. In essence, I rose from the superficialities of self-esteem issues to the more mature requirements of self-respect.

Sooner or later, other issues will assuredly rise, causing consternation—whether on a personal, family or professional level. But I hope I will now be better-equipped to deal with such occurrences—knowing, now, that there is a way out of anything.

Success today, I measure differently than yesterday. Because of the past few years of chaos, I know it to be founded on being fully present in the now; compassionate, loving, generous, serene and joyful. But to achieve all of that and maintain its powers, is a daily chore, a choice, a priority.

If this illness makes me a better person, if it allows me to help others in similar circumstances, then it will have been all worthwhile.

I no longer seek to save the world but rather to sow joy and love through small daily gestures. I try to recognize and appreciate the talents with which I have been blessed and to put them to use in the service of others—and this in all simplicity and humility.

In recent past times, my horror stories would repeat themselves endlessly—both at night and during the day—and this, in the darkest corners of what was then my soul. It is through putting words to those images, by giving myself a voice, that I was able to begin to heal. Through this sharing of words that open a door to a better world for me, I hope to gain a resonance, a connection with the images and words of others.

Naturally, my approach to healing is very personal. There is no one route to health but rather many roads that lead us to the same place—an area where the scars may still be present, but less visible; an area where there is much more light than darkness. When we begin listening to our bodies and souls, it is possible to discover what needs to be heard and how to better listen. And sometimes . . . the decision to take on the demons that assail us can come from reading about the experiences of others.

Mental illness remains a difficult topic to deal with, despite its prevalence in all societies. Sadly, it seems to be even more common than in the past. And whether we admit to it or not, we are all vulnerable. For that matter, we all know at least one person who is dealing with it, and yet . . . speaking up remains difficult.

Too many, touched by PTSD, remain in its shadow: soldiers, local and international aid workers, policemen and women, journalists, firefighters and all other first-responders . . .

Solitude may be a wonderful place where we can enjoy our own company. But loneliness, of the magnitude of those who suffer from PTSD, is where everyone is lost, where no one can be found—not even the sufferer.

And it is in the loneliness of a personal mental health battle that despair grows. In a world where human contact and connection is less and less tangible, where self-isolation becomes an insurmountable challenge, the world's sufferers need a whisper of hope, support and caring. But then, we all do.

What we all need is to find a voice; our voice; that voice which has the courage to say what we so desperately need it to say in order that our hearts be cleansed of that which needs to be erased.

We must give to all suffering in silence the chance to free themselves, the chance to live again.

Chapter 9: Beyond Post-Traumatic Stress Disorder

And relationships?

An open heart

Autumn 2015

It has been over five years since I first put pen to paper. The process of writing and sharing has shown me that we all have unlimited potential to learn; to go beyond the impossible.

Living life fully happens gradually. It is easier to sometimes avoid situations and to procrastinate with potential triggers that may still feel threatening and frightening. There was a time when these triggers could have created much havoc in our lives. Now they may still disturb without sending us into a deep negative spiral. Moving forward, it is important to realize that when these situations recur, we can tame the fears and move beyond them.

Fear can lead to a variety of emotions, including anxiety and anger . . . It is natural to want to protect ourselves. Nonetheless, we must learn to control these emotions rather than submit to them. They must become learning opportunities rather than be the cause of difficult-to-deal-with pain. I was inspired by Michael Singer's book *The Untethered Soul*.[19] He leads us to focus on the opening-up of our heart. Though we must acknowledge that on occasion and despite our best efforts, it may still tighten up—even close up—our emphasis should not be on the fact that it does but rather on getting it re-opened again as soon as possible.

"In essence, the goal is to gain control over hurtful emotions—to use them as purifiers of the heart. By reversing their power polarity;

---

[19] Singer, Michael, *The Untethered Soul,* New Harbinger Publications Inc., Oakland, USA, 2007

by taking over where they once forced us to submit, we chance gaining a level of strength that, when put into gear, affords us the power to fight the closing up of our hearts—and this through a renewable source of positive energy."

I choose to call this energy: LOVE and COMPASSION. And this combo, through our words and presence in the lives of others, is a contagious alliance. And as a self-energizing source of connection, it lays the foundation for love and contentment to grow both within us and within those we connect with.

To achieve such a personal soul strength, daily meditation is a potential aide. It sets us on a path that takes us beyond the difficulties we encounter, thus helping us recognize the universal characteristics-of suffering. And through this familiarization, the suffering of others can also be more easily recognized and dealt with.

Meditating on compassion is a traditional Buddhist practice. It heightens the establishment of feelings of goodness towards both ourselves and others. The following directions can assist in establishing such a daily practice in our lives:

1- Begin by sitting in a comfortable chair. To promote relaxation and encourage interior calm, take a few minutes to focus on our inhaling and exhaling breaths. If a thought enters our mind, we should recognize it as being there and simply let it pass.

2- The actual meditation involves repeating the following phrases—allowing for whatever images and feelings they elicit to come to the fore:

> May, that I be filled with goodness
> May, that I be happy
> May, that I be healthy
> May, that I be in peace

3- Once we achieve a level of compassion in regards to ourselves, it becomes possible to include others in this practice. To encourage this direction, we can begin by including a benevolent someone (a teacher, mentor or family member), a friend, an unknown person whose path we may have crossed but whose name we do not know. The goal, eventually, is to include even the name of someone with whom we may have had or have a difficult relationship. The phrases then are:

> May, that he/she be filled with goodness
> May, that he/she be happy
> May, that he/she be healthy
> May, that he/she be in peace

The idea is to begin with a 15-minute meditation, progressing to (ideally) a daily 30 minute session.

Empathy

Communication is something that must be worked on daily. To successfully communicate, we must be open to another. This implies allowing ourselves to be vulnerable. At the heart of communication lies respect and empathy.

Empathetic communication does not require we find solutions for another nor does it need for us to solve another's problems. Brené Brown, PhD clearly explains the difference between sympathy and empathy. "Empathy nourishes connection with another. Sympathy disconnects us from each other. Empathy is a sacred bond between two people. It acknowledges that we know of and respect another's situation; be it problematic or positive. Our vulnerability is the key that allows us to both connect with and feel for another without overwhelming that other's feelings with ours."

In her book, *I Thought It Was Just Me,*[20] she describes the four components of empathy:

1- Acknowledge the other's perspective of their truth
2- Stay away from judgments
3- Recognize the emotions of the other
4- Communicate our recognition of the other's experienced emotions

Vulnerability

In the art of opening up to others, I needed to overcome a handicap, a handicap called shame. I was ashamed of having a mental health problem. I was ashamed of being defective, inept, troubled. After a year of therapy, it was finally possible for me to slowly begin the process. I first opened up to my neighbour.

Realistically, there isn't much difference between a physical and a mental illness. But, also realistically, a stigma still exists in certain segments of society and sometimes in workplaces. Some of us become silent or frightened when confronted by those who are sometimes muted or frightened by mental health issues. For us it is a question of what can I say? What will they think? How will it affect my work, my relationships?

In her book, *Daring Greatly,*[21] Brené Brown describes the four elements of resilience when faced with shame:

1. **Recognizing Shame and Understanding Its Triggers.** Shame is biology and biography. Can we physically recognize when we are in the grips of shame, feel our way through it, and figure out what messages and expectations triggered it?
2. **Practicing Critical Awareness.** Can we reality-check the messages and expectations that are driving our shame? Are

---

[20] Brown, Brené, PhD, *I Thought It Was Just Me,* Penguin Group, New York, USA, 2007
[21] Brown, Brené, PhD, *Daring Greatly*, Penguin Group, New York, USA, 2012

they realistic? Attainable? Are they what we want to be or what we think others need/want from us?
3. **Reaching Out.** Are we owning and sharing our story? We can't experience empathy if we are not connecting.
4. **Speaking Shame.** Are we talking about how we feel and asking for what we need when we feel shame?

In order to move forward, to reach a level of resilience that can not only handle but face down shame, it would be advisable to review weekly the four elements of resilience as described above. While absorbing them, it would be a good time to think back upon that previous week to see if there were any situations that caused shame to reinstate itself. And finally, every weekend is a good time to ask ourselves where we are in light of empathy for our own selves.

As Brené Brown states: practicing resilience helps to contextualize (see the overall situation), normalize (take us out of solitude) and demystify (share our insight on the topic with others).

Shame is a topic all on its own. It needs to be looked into since shame is a serious braking mechanism. It prevents many from coming forward, from coming out of the shadows. Though I want to say loud and clear that there is no shame in having to deal with mental health issues... That is what I say now. That is what I promote as a message now... But to get to that head space I spent many hours, days and months isolated from the fresh air of freedom. I therefore recommend highly the above regular review as an encouragement; as a stimulant exercise; as a normalizing potion.

If we can take a serious look, a serious stand regarding shame, if we arrive at a stage where outing it, discussing it and understanding it becomes normalized, we will avoid both the contemplation and actions taken in regards to suicide. In essence, it is not the emotional distress, the upset that becomes impossible to endure. It is the all-encompassing feelings of being alone that kills.

All of us need to "know" that we are not alone. All of us need to be able to identify and recognize those who are "there" ready for us when and if need be; be they family, friends or professional resources. All of us need a place where we can be vulnerable and not feel panicked, where our stories can be told without rejection and our feelings validated. We all need a secure environment where being listened to does not feel as if we are burdening someone else. We need a place where courage will overpower fears, blame be transformed into compassion and feelings of isolation and rejection become respectful connections. And finally, the greatest benefit of reaching out and sharing is the realization that isolation and shame are universal sentiments whose crushing weight is lessened through connection.

Communication

Through workshops and support groups that I conduct, I often highlight the importance of good communication in all spheres of life. Here is a summary of the principles of non-violent communication as put forth by Marshall B. Rosenberg, PhD. The goals presented emphasize the two elements of communication: the expressor and the receiver and how we share and perceive communications of another.

OBSERVATION—

The first step in non-violent communication consists of observing without judgment or criticism. Humans have a tendency to see and analyze through their own specific prism, which, when utilized in difficult circumstances, may deviate or deform reality.

FEELINGS—

The second step is to begin expressing our reactions and feelings through "I feel" not by saying "I think." The best way to have our sentiments understood by others is to clearly share "our" feelings with them.

NEEDS—

The third step is to recognize what our own needs are and to express them. The idea is to state clearly what we need without necessarily imposing how those needs should be realized.

REQUESTS—

The last step in non-violent communication lies in the formulating of a clear request. The idea, first hand, is to recognize that others cannot be expected to read our minds as to what constitutes our needs. And once a concrete request is posted, we accept that the outcome is based on the other's capacity or willingness to acquiesce to the request.

Oftentimes, a healing process is long and drawn out, and triggers continue to hinder family relationships. The following is a tool that might improve communications and identify specific needs.

Toolbox for Family Communication[22]

Re: person suffering from PTSD

Possible situations or causes of TRIGGERED reactions:

Loud noises
A crowded place (restaurant, department store)
Someone walking fast
Position in room (my back to the room)
Children crying
Other_____

When I am triggered, what I need from my loved ones:

Acknowledgment
To be touched—OR NOT to be touched
To be left alone—OR NOT to be left alone
Other_____

Family Members

When you are triggered, this is how I feel:

Alone
Abandoned
Worried

Shut-out

---

[22] "Triggers and How to Cope with Them" spring 2011 newsletter, www.OSISS.ca

Angry
Helpless
Other _____

When you are triggered, what I need from you:

Acknowledgement
Verbal cues (are you leaving, how long will you be gone, are you okay?)
Tell me what might help you
If we were discussing an issue, I need to know that we will address it later
Other _____

Boundaries

Good fences make good neighbours. They should neither be too restricting nor too loose. Caregiving, as it relates to a family member and/or any person with health issues, can often be too loose in the area of limits or fences. This is a personal observation as it affected me greatly while in Africa.

Those who respect a balanced limits framework, seem to be those who have the ability to offer and accept help when required, who take responsibility for their own happiness and who expect the same of others in regards to their contentment. They do not feel responsible for the feelings or needs of others and do not neglect their own needs. They have a distinct self-identity that differentiates them from others and very comfortably are capable of saying "no" when required.

The above paragraph is definitely food for thought in regards to participating in cooperative work involving humanitarian aid. This also goes for those who wish to accompany individuals who suffer, whether physically or mentally. Learning to establish healthy boundaries (and this without guilt) is a whole process in and of itself. Therefore requesting help from a counselor or group, before and during these activities, is not only a wise move, it is crucial.

And now, what about managing physical, mental and emotional health?

The nervous system

In our much too fast and furious (it seems) societies and cultures, it is more often than not better to communicate "energetic calm." And, according to Rick Hanson, PhD and Daniel J. Siegel, MD in *Buddha's Brain*,[23] an optimal balance in this area can be achieved through the activation of our parasympathetic (Rest and Digest) nervous system and by moderately activating our sympathetic nervous system (Fight or Flight).

In other words, it is better to choose contemplative or calming influences rather than those that generate overly passionate or overly enthusiastic responses. This is not to say that such a quest is easily achievable in an era of over-stimulation and high speed rhythms.

For more than three years, I have treated patients using reflexology to help manage stress. It is evident to me that alternative therapies and such other activities as tai-chi, yoga, gardening, painting, reading, listening to music, progressive body relaxation, visualization, meditation, acupuncture, etc. do play a role in balancing the automatic nervous system (i.e., by activating the parasympathetic side of things).

Breathing

Simple breathing techniques do increase the amounts of oxygen being directed to the brain. And this helps bring about a more balanced nervous system. Added benefits? Revitalization of the body, regulation of emotional expressions and a clear mind.

---

[23] Hanson, Rick, PhD and Mendius, Richard, MD, *Buddha's Brain*, New Harbinger Publications, Oakland, USA, 2009

Breathing-in by the rule of 6 (as recommended by a psychologist):

1- Begin by sitting comfortably in a chair. Close your eyes.
2- Breathe deeply from the abdomen, filling the belly area as you would a basketball. Take in air using long breaths through the nose. Count to 6.
3- Hold your breath and count to 6.
4- Exhale through the mouth—slowly—counting to 6.
5- Repeat 6 times.
6- Repeat daily—morning, noon and night or as required.

I have simplified the following alternative yoga breathing exercise in order to meet the needs of more people. I find this exercise to be most beneficial during times of stress or agitation.

1- Begin by sitting comfortably in a chair.
2- Breathe deeply from the abdomen, filling the belly area as you would a basketball. Inhale through the left nostril—blocking the right with your thumb as you inhale. Hold to the count of 8.
3- Block both nostrils to the count of 8.
4- Exhale through the right nostril while blocking the left. Try to stretch the exhale to the count of 16 if possible.
5- Alternate. (Breathe through the right nostril while blocking the left. Inhale to the count of 8.)
6- Hold and block both nostrils to the count of 8.
7- Exhale through the left nostril; blocking the right. Try to extend exhale to the count of 16 if possible.
8- Repeat the exercise for 15 minutes.

Exercise

Exercise is an important exercise (no pun intended) in the maintenance of a balanced nervous system. For some it is even crucial. According to Men's Harvard Watch, 30 minutes of physical exercise per day is basic. During that amount of time, physical activities reduce stress related hormones and increase levels of well-being endorphins. Sleep, in scheduled adequate amounts, is also indispensable in the regeneration of both mind and body strength.

Managing thoughts and emotions

Once interior conflicts subside, a letting go, a feeling of wellness emerges. An acceptance of what is, what was and what may be tomorrow arises and calm bids us rest.

Being ever more fully conscious, being mindful, for all intents and purposes "thinking" takes on new dimensions. Thinking takes up more and more space in our lives. And with that, choices . . . Do we choose to pay more attention to our projects, our dreams? Or do we instead focus on our problems?

It is a given. Most of us prefer living in a state of harmony with the world. But sometimes we find our well-being more dependent on that which is without than that which is within (i.e., on our surroundings, our work, our leisure time). But whether we are aware of it or not, well-being comes from within. And from within, thoughts of a varying nature constantly emerge during any given day. Managing our thoughts, therefore, is a priority. They play a major role in our well-being, and so a significant way of dealing with thoughts must be found. Mindfulness can play an important role in this area. With time and practice, meditation as an exercise can teach us detachment—the art of taking a step back in order to analyze the contents of a thought and its linked situations.

What would happen if there was a possibility of applying this process to our daily lives, to our beliefs, to our perceptions, to our definitions of reality? We just might discover how more accepting we can be towards ourselves and towards others. Nonetheless, there is a problem. And that problem, in this flexibility of consideration, is "reason." In western civilizations, reason is a staple. Despite the fact that it can be wrong in one circumstance or another, we tend to trust it unequivocally. Many of us are convinced that our reality, our perceptions, our beliefs, our values, our experiences are the only valid ones that can be considered. And yet . . .

The management of not only thoughts but also of perceptions is an almost full-time job. But then we can, if we wish, change our modus operandi. We can alter our current perceptions of a difficult situation by changing prisms, by changing our glasses to better focus on that which we wish to create in our lives. Naturally, this takes practice. Eventually, by defining the new perceptions we wish to adopt, as well as the corresponding imagery and feelings, refocusing becomes possible. Through daily commitment of creating new neural pathways in the brain, we realize that, in the end, this process sustains personal growth and positive change in our lives.

I can vouch for this meditative process (Dr. Joe Dispenza, *Breaking the Habit of Being Yourself*), for humans have the possibility of generating new opportunities through changing the way they think. Spending time and energy changing thought patterns and perceptions has offered me much in the area of opportunities and energy.

And so, if we give mindfulness a go, how is this tool used in the simplest form possible? When I do dishes, when I drive a car, when I am walking from point A to point B, where do I, can I focus my attention? Where are my thoughts? Are they in the past, in the future or in the present? Can I return to this moment through my body and the natural rhythm of my breathing in and out?

Sometimes I imagine myself sitting in the chair of my consciousness, whereupon I am staring at a computer screen filled with a flood of thoughts, visual and otherwise. If I choose to connect to and surf the Internet, it is easy to get lost. My computer is connected to a satellite and as I surf, the satellite emits signals. The signals that my satellite receives are projected outwards and can disturb the weather as it does its thing. And so, I compare this scenario with emotions and their consequences. This "vision" reminds me to regularly review my thoughts and emotions. What I try to do is acknowledge them, but to not get too caught up in them. I learn through this review to not try to control or resist my thoughts or feelings but rather to let them pass while staying open and receptive.

The following acronym, RAIN, as described by Dan Harris in his book: *10% Happier*[24] can be used as a daily mindfulness tool to manage emotions.

Recognize the emotion: acknowledge the feeling.

Allow the emotion to present itself, to exist. Let it be. Lean into it. Offer the inner whisper of "yes."

Investigate how the emotion is affecting my body. Is it making my face hot, my chest buzzy, my head throb?

Non-identification: Seeing that just because I am feeling angry or jealous or fearful, that does not render me a permanently angry or jealous person. These are just passing states of mind.

If we go back to my Internet analogy: The satellite may emit a disturbing signal based on the information it receives from the Internet (my feelings). But as storms arrive, they also pass. The sun eventually shines again.

As long as an emotion is not too debilitating, I welcome it. I observe it. I let it pass. When possible, I try to live through its impact on my own. Immediately trying to explain it to someone is too difficult since it often takes on overwhelming proportions: the sadness incurred is intensified and the guilt too intense, leading to further emotional turmoil in need of handling.

In his book, *You Are Here*,[25] the peace activist and spiritual leader Thich Nhat Hanh suggests we visualize ourselves as a tree. During a

---

[24] Harris, Dan, *10% Happier*, Dey Street Books, New York, USA, 2014

storm, winds play havoc with branches and leaves. Yet, our tree trunk remains calm, solid, rooted. It therefore behooves us to return to our core essence, our trunk. With a focus on regulated breathing we can allow the storm to pass, calm to return and the sun to shine, before considering taking any further steps.

Sometimes, though, we are faced with a situation that demands reasoning before we take on a regulated breathing session. In other words, when faced with a too difficult situation, I have been recommended the following:

Transforming Emotions by Modifying Thoughts

Translating thought processes

(exercise is taken from the book Mind Over Mood[26] *by Dennis Greenberger, PhD and Christine A. Padesky, PhD)*

In chapter 5, I outlined a 2012 meeting that I had with a rehabilitation counselor. Intense feelings erupted during this discussion. The feelings that overtook me were so intense and debilitating, objectivity of vision was impossible. I was transported by our conversation into a devastating past and could not extract myself from that past. I needed an efficient tool to regain my footing and stability.

The following exercise is an example of how the thought record described in the book *Mind over Mood* can be applied:

---

[25] Hanh, Thich Nhat, *You Are Here*, Shambhala Publications Inc., Boston, USA, 2009

[26] 7-column Thought Record used from *Mind Over Mood* is copyrighted by Christine A. Padesky (copyright 1983) and reprinted with permission (reference: Dennis Greenberger, PhD and Christine A. Padesky, PhD, *Mind Over Mood: Change How You Feel by Changing the Way You Think*, Second Edition, The Guilford Press, New York, USA, 2016)

1. Situation
Who were you with? *My psychologist and the re-adaptation specialist hired by the insurance company.*
What were you doing? *I was discussing the possibility of returning back to work. At the end of the meeting, I became very emotional and could not continue our conversation. I felt triggered when the re-adaptation specialist brought forth the subject of the meeting with the psychiatrist (evaluator) in Montreal.*
When was it? *January 31st 2012*
Where were you? *In my psychologist's office*
2. Moods
Describe each mood in one word. Rate intensity of the mood (0-100 %)
Fear (80%) *Anxiety (100%)* *Powerlessness (80%)*   *Anger (50%)* *Despair (90%)*
3. Automatic Thoughts (images)
What was going through my mind just before I started feeling this way? *Insurance companies are in it for the money and not for the well-being of the insured. This is so unjust. I don't trust this process.*
What does this mean about me? My life? My future? *I do not have the energy to fight and justify my case with the insurance company anymore. My financial future is compromised.*
What am I afraid might happen? *I am afraid of never being able to go back to work.*
What is the worst thing that could happen if this is true? *I would perhaps eventually have to sell our home and move with my family into low-*

rental housing.

What does this mean about how the other person(s) feel(s)/ think(s) about me? *The rehabilitation specialist does not understand my psychological state. PTSD and depression do not show as a physical illness does. She is here to convey the message. The insurance company is not interested in paying long-term benefits. In four months, I will have to come up with yet more proof I am inapt for work.*

What does this mean about the other person(s) or people in general? *Insurance businesses are often self-serving. In that light, I cannot trust them.*

What images or memories do I have in this situation? *Images of the meeting in the office of the psychiatrist, feeling totally powerless and at the mercy of his decision.*

4. Evidence that Supports the Hot Thought

Circle hot thought in previous column for which you are looking for evidence *I am afraid of never being able to go back to work.*

Write factual evidence to support this conclusion (try to avoid mind-reading and interpretation of facts)

I am not able to drive too close to the place I was working when I was diagnosed with PTSD.

I still encounter triggers on a frequent basis related to Africa, the separation with my ex-husband and work.

I am still undergoing psychological treatment for complex PTSD (EMDR).

5. Evidence that Does Not Support the Hot Thought
(I am afraid of never being able to go back to work.)

Questions to help find evidence that does not support your hot thought

Have I had any experiences that show that this thought is not

completely true all the time? *I have been able to do some writing and research in the past few months. I am working on a book. My concentration seems to be getting progressively better.*

If my best friend or someone I loved had this thought, what would I tell them? *Trust in your capacities. You have come such a long way. I believe you will be able to recover.*

When I am not feeling this, do I still think of this type of situation differently? How? *I think of this situation in a more positive light and I believe I can get back to work eventually.*

When I have felt this way in the past, what did I think about that helped me feel better? *I think about what I have control over (inner world), what I can do to make myself better and not that which I have no control over (outer world).*

Five years from now, if I look back at this situation, will I look at it any differently? Will I focus on any different part of my experience? *Perhaps I would see my strength in overcoming all the obstacles that I had to face.*

Are there any strengths or positives in me or the situation that I am ignoring? *My perseverance, my commitment to recovery, the great support from family and friends.*

Am I jumping to any conclusions in column 3 and 4 that are not completely justified by evidence? *My perception of the insurance company and their consultants.*

Other questions:

Am I blaming myself for something over which I do not have complete control?

If my best friend or someone who loves me knew I was thinking this thought, what would they say to me? What evidence would they point out to me that would suggest that my thoughts were not 100% true?

Have I been in this type of situation before? What happened? Is there anything different between this situation and previous ones? What have I learned from prior experiences that could help me now?

Are there any small things that contradict my thoughts that I might be discounting as not important?

6. Alternate/balanced thinking:

Ask yourself the following questions to generate alternative or balanced thoughts:

Based on the evidence I have listed in columns 4 and 5 of the Thought Record, is there an alternative way of thinking about or understanding the situation?

Write one sentence that summarizes all the evidence that supports my hot thought (column 4) and all the evidence that does not support my hot thought (column 5). Does combining the two summary statements with the word "and" create a balanced thought that takes into account all the information I have gathered?

If someone I cared about was in this situation, had these thoughts, and had this information available, what would be my advice to them? How would I suggest that they understand the situation?

If my hot thought is true, what is the worst outcome? If my hot thought is true, what is the best outcome? If my hot thought is true, what is the most realistic outcome?

Can someone I trust think of any other way of understanding this situation?

Write an alternative or balanced thought

Even though I have not yet fully recovered, I have made progress. Perhaps I will not be able to work full-time, but I could at the very least take a part

> *time job that does not require too much concentration to begin with.*
>
> **Rate how much you believe in your alternative balanced thought.**
>
> *75%*

---

7. Rate Moods Now

Copy the feelings from Column 2. Rerate the intensity of each feeling from 0 to 100% as well as any new records.

Fear (25%)   Anxiety (50%)

Powerlessness (25%)   Anger (10%)   Despair (25%)

The tool chest

We often are ill-prepared to deal with life's serious challenges. And sometimes we forget to take the time to arm ourselves with the necessary tools to deal with maintaining our well-being. In the garage or the basement or in a closet we all have a tool chest; screwdrivers, pliers, hammers and saws . . .

So what is in our mental health tool chest? What tool in that chest can provide us with the wherewithal to do "repairs" to our well-being? WRAP, the (Wellness Recovery Action Plan)—available at the following address: www.mentalhealthrecovery.com/wrap-is/ offers up an action plan, as a guide not only to the assortment of tools required but also as a help to identify those triggers that might do damage to our "foundation."

Creativity

One of the greatest tools that all humans have, and this from birth, is a capacity to be creative. Creativity is a blessed thing. It is both boundless and endless. It fits any and all activities if we give it the power to do so. Its special quality is that it can take the ordinary and make it extraordinary.

In my case I have taken on a mission, an action plan. Whether intended or not, the diagnosis I lived with has shaped the structure of my days, months and years, of my life. And this structure has led me to a decision: sow the well-being I have encountered in the souls of others. This decision is open-ended. It has few restrictions. It allows me to both reach out and comfort others while encouraging myself to meet further challenges head on.

As the months go by, defining a personal mission of ours based on our values, skills, talents and interests can slowly, gradually shape itself through determination. I believe that two important factors of recovery are perception and action. Looking at this health challenge as an opportunity to contribute to society and to others redefines it more as a valuable experience rather than a devastating defeat. Through defining a personal mission, a code of honour that guides our daily actions, we can gain a beautiful sense of contribution and connection. Eventually we may feel even comfortable enough to actually allow the universe to play a role in that redefinition of our "self"—both physically and emotionally.

And through this act of reaching out, of providing mutual support, of sharing and caring, the cost of PTSD . . . just maybe . . . might prove itself to have been a human gain.

Annex 1

Observations regarding international development and humanitarian aid work

The dream of living an international cooperation experience or a humanitarian aid mission should begin with a voyage of exploration of ourselves. Discovering who we are is crucial before embarking on an adventure with so many unknowns. The idea is to evaluate, analyze and ask the right questions, such as: What are my options? Am I really ready to go on such a quest?

From the beginning, it is crucial to know what the details are concerning the mandate and context of the work being considered. It is also important to question how well we are prepared to handle potentially encountered stresses. Are we aware of the symptoms (and how to deal with them) that might appear both during and after a project has ended and we are back at home?

Vigilance

When a traumatic episode occurs, an individual must be able to deal with the several arising situations, and this, rapidly. Adapting to extremes can surpass a body's, a head's, a spirit's ability to cope. Also, reactions to a return home can be just as traumatic. We must learn to reintegrate with our social milieu, our work environment and even a new climate. In essence, it is a lot to deal with all at once. For some it may be an overwhelming challenge, if not an impossible one. Too strong demands on a psyche can manifest themselves either physically, mentally or both. Professional help specialized in the identification of traumatic stress and its relief is at times required to manage occurring symptoms.

In the *Humanitarian Exchange Magazine,*[27] Peter Solama casts a

---

[27] Solama Peter, *Humanitarian Exchange Magazine*, Issue 15, Psychological Health

light on a variety of reactions that are commonly observed in humanitarian aid workers who are not treated for stress related symptoms. "Upon his or her return from a mission abroad, a worker, in a quest to regain control, may display subtle changes in their behavior. Some individuals react through feelings of guilt and/or feelings of overly strong identification with individuals or a population being or having been assisted. In equal and opposite measure, some distance themselves completely—as is evidenced in more experienced workers. Individuals who distance themselves from traumatic events also feel a distancing within themselves and with their personal and/or home environment. Such persons can display self-destructive behaviors such as over-working to a point of total exhaustion, excessive alcohol or drug consumption or dangerous (unprotected) sex."

A—Factors that contribute to stress

If we use me as an example, the essentials of the experienced stress are attributable to several factors.

- **Living conditions**: Suffocating heat, insufficient and inconsistent water availability, no basic sanitary infrastructure, no functional sewers, overwhelming smells on a daily basis, incessant noise from morning 'til night, innumerable varied insects roaming the residence throughout the night.

- **Separation from family and friends**: Through illnesses and varied difficulties emanating from the humanitarian aid mission, the unfathomable distance of family and friends cannot be discounted. Emails, telephone calls often cannot compensate for the lack of a physical presence. Months pass without a "concrete" contact, and this engenders great difficulties in the eventual reintegration to our homeland and once fluid connections.

-**Lack of personal space, of intimacy and basic comforts**: Africa is another world, another lifestyle, existence. It is a world of family and tribal customs. There is little if any room for individuality or personal comforts. Life in such an environment is made up of closeness 24 hours a day. Compound guards and housemaids know of every coming and going because in such an environment nothing goes unnoticed or unheard.

- **Relationship difficulties in the workplace**: Africa is a world where men are proud of their stature and family. As a white woman, sharing knowledge and taking one's place in their society is not as easy as it might appear to be. Destabilizing "what is" has consequences, and egos are easily bruised. With no knowledge of the local language, it is difficult to connect, to converse and to understand what and how things must be done.

- **Lack of leisure activities**: In rural areas there are no cinemas, no pools that have treated or healthy water, no restaurants other than local food. In the first weeks after arrival, the world is all new and attractive and eagerly embraced. After a few months, a quest to find "something" to do other than work is difficult.

- **Lack of medical facilities and service infrastructures seem to enhance a serious risk of accidents and illness**: Every small headache, each discomfort becomes a worry. Is it nothing but a passing virus or is it malaria? Despite every hygienic precaution, for example: disinfecting fruits and vegetables after returning from the marketplace and only consuming fresh meat, intestinal parasites remain difficult to avoid.

- **Road accidents**: Again in Africa, hitting the roads is an informed chance taken. More people die in road accidents than of illness. In serious accidents, the worst is not necessarily the event but rather having no competent or secure medical service to tend to the damage. The risk of finding oneself in a contaminated public hospital is high. Where operations are unavoidable, doctors prefer flying out expatriate patients to other countries where risk of complications is less elevated.

- **Threat to personal stability**: Without an environment that can provide good sleep facilities, good rest potential, personal space, facilities to exercise and be oneself, mental health can be and is at times threatened.

- **Exposure to constant suffering of others:** The impossibility to respond to the needs of suffering people can be seriously traumatic—especially when it is a matter of such basics as no money, no medication, no understanding or appreciation of the devastating factors involved in an illness such as HIV. Intentions are well and good, but when nothing else is available, the results are often devastatingly discouraging to an aid worker.

For many international development and humanitarian aid workers, the challenges are considerable and stress factors great. Due to cultural imperatives, ambiguity of events and expectations are often convoluted. Workloads are often heavy, communication difficult, security non-existent and corruption inevitable.

B—Stress related to arrivals in foreign lands and to a return to home base is often under-estimated.

International development and humanitarian aid workers are often stressed from the very outset. They are going to an unknown land where the climate is often hostile. They are far from family and friends and at times far from help if and when help is drastically needed.

Returning home, to a "normal" life, represents another challenge as re-connecting with family and friends can be difficult. Comprehension of what has been experienced is rarely palpable as those who remained home know nothing of the difficulties encountered. Being home also means financial instability and lack of resources for future employment.

International development and humanitarian aid work can be a rich and positive experience for those who have a profile that is compatible with intercultural experience accompanied by a high capacity for adaptation to unknown environments and situations. Someone else who would have lived my experience could have lived it completely differently. And this is where a realistic perspective, serious analysis and research before a departure are crucial. Being well-prepared will most likely guarantee a successful sojourn in another land and culture. Ignoring these preliminary steps may shatter a dream and possibly be dangerous to both mental and physical health.

To give wings to our hopes and aspirations, the reading of *The Enneagram*[28]: *Understanding Yourself and the Others in Your Life* by Helen Palmer allows for insight into our own personalities. It opens the door to a better comprehension of our strengths and weaknesses.

Following the reading of *The Enneagram*, do I recognize myself in any of these personality types?

If I scan my personal history, as to both personal and professional experiences, how would I measure my stress management skills?

What are my real motivations regarding international development or humanitarian aid?

What is driving me to leave home and work for others in foreign lands?

Am I running away from some recent event in my life that could be tainting my motives?

Am I going off to far flung places for the right reasons?

During my past travels, how did I do in the area of adaptation? Did I adjust well to unfamiliar places?

---

[28] Palmer, Helen, *The Enneagram: Understanding Yourself and the Others in Your Life*, HarperCollins Publishers, USA, 1991.

What problems did I encounter?

What are my coping mechanisms? Are they healthy?

What did I learn from my mistakes?

Am I the right fit for such work?

Based on my personality, my limitations and my strengths, will such an adventure build on or destroy my potential?

Do I tend to take on other people's problems as my own?

Am I blessed with good physical and mental health?

Adaptation

Adaptation to Foreign Lands

After several months, I was finally able to function despite the stress related to culture chock and the desperate living conditions I was experiencing. Nonetheless, adaptation was my biggest enemy. Before the departure for Africa, I became aware of this. But I had no idea how intense that incapacity was.

If, before my adventure, I had taken the time to better study the culture of the *Burkinabé*. If I had spent time with Africans from Burkina Faso living in Canada—communicating with them, seeking their opinions and advice—it would assuredly have been easier for me to adapt. If I had taken a more comprehensive course on international cooperation rather than a simple overview session, what would have my capacities revealed? If I had researched where I would be living and how, would that not have improved my time there and reduced the stress encountered? If I had assured myself a solid support base upon my arrival and return to Canada, would life have been better in Africa? If I had better planned my encounter with the *Burkinabé* would have they better profited and me too from my interventions? If I had prepared a return formula ahead of time, based on activities and projects once home... maybe the whole situation would have been just as bad but I would have been better prepared to handle it all.

Before leaving for Africa, during my pre-departure international development training sessions, I did an inventory of my intercultural adaptation capacities. The list of points laid out is the following: open to new experiences, sociable and have an appreciation of differences. Am flexible, tolerant when encountering ambiguity, persistent, self-confident, emotionally stable and autonomous as a personality.

My head said I was ready, open and flexible for this experience. But when I was confronted with different life demands and social expectations, I soon realized there was a huge gulf between my self-analysis and the realities being lived. And that added enormously to the amount of stress I ended up dealing with.

Beyond knowing oneself, there is also self-respect and basic personal requirements that need to be taken into account. These considerations need to be deeply looked into before making serious major changes to our lives. For example, in a country where the intercultural imperatives are tribal, an individual in need of solitude will definitely be confronted with intercultural expectations and limitations.

Well-prepared, such a venture can be most rewarding for all concerned. Activities of this kind are not only an opportunity to get to know others but also to discover ourselves. Often, we end up receiving more than we have given. It is in the recognition and acceptance of cultural differences that we rise to the greater that we can be. The only criteria? We must be well-prepared.

Adapting to coming home

Adapting to Africa and its demands is a seemingly obvious one thing. Returning home is another just as demanding (if not more) expedition. How do we face and surmount the difficulties encountered, including culture shock, upon returning home? The honeymoon is quickly over hence a return to "our" old ways and lives.

Upon their return, international development and humanitarian aid workers have possibly already exhausted their quota of physical and psychological resources. Re-adapting to home, re-integrating old social circles, finding work, establishing a new and most different routine, adapting to new weather, physical spaces, family connections and social values—everything is different and challenging, "again."

The feeling of suddenly being on "empty" is inevitable. In a developing country expats are often perceived to be potential "saviors." They are placed on a pedestal whose stature is at times blushingly embarrassing. At baptisms, weddings and funerals, they are offered the best chairs. They are invited to dine before all others are served. Back home, these same "saviors" must reinvent themselves. They must abandon their adopted superior persona, in order to better fit their "ordinary" (read: real) status.

Melancholy may set in. Saying goodbye to those with whom we had been closely tied for many months is not easy.

Upon our return it is important to take the time to explain, to share, to describe the time spent "there," to speak of the people encountered and the land visited. As well, it is good to take care of ourselves by planning; by reviewing the experience had, by facing the future with a balanced and organized plan, and by consulting regarding prospective activities—both personal and potentially professional.

Going off as a couple

The rate of separation and divorce is considerably high in those couples who choose to head off to work in other lands as humanitarian aid workers. Alone, the challenges are already great. As a couple, they double in complexity and impact. For some, sharing such an experience can be a mutually supportive adventure, with the quest bringing them closer. But many unknown or unexpected elements can occur, playing havoc with the integrity of any couple.

Work "overseas" is often related to management crises, emergencies, unexpected situations and events. Research takes on new meaning when the adventurers are a couple. How does a couple cope with a crisis—as a couple? When our reaction mechanisms differ profoundly, as normally they do in individuals; our adaptation capacities do also. Crises and how they are handled as a couple can determine and even interfere in a couple's intimacy and everyday functioning. It is already difficult to find the means and the wherewithal to take care of our own needs. But when a couple's needs "need satisfaction" the solution to that (in another world, culture and environment) can be difficult to find.

It is therefore seriously important to measure the health of a couple before undertaking such a drastic measure as living and working in an unknown environment.

When a world is filled with unclear if not strange directives, it is rarely easy to take a stand, find a position from which we, as a pair, can determine outcomes. What is that person of this new culture trying to communicate? How should I respond when I am not sure how to—based on my lack of knowledge regarding this culture? I thought I understood what was being planned, but once on the field of action I realize I did not. How do I deal with that as an individual? How do I deal with this as a couple? I underestimated my capacity to adapt. Once there, how do I deal with this and other situations? What do "I" do? As a couple, what do "we" do? Being alone is not easy. Being two, oddly, can be even more difficult. Being strangers in a strange land is never more obvious and complex.

At times, living spaces are cramped. But even when possible, leaving that tiny space to "get some air" is restricted. Inside the confined area, there are always others. Outside that space we again are also surrounded. Finding a healthy balance for the survival of a couple's needs can slowly, eerily, become rather impossible.

In essence, renouncing comfort and intimacy is almost a must in some postings—as dangerous as that may be to the survival of a "western" marriage ... Optimal conditions are at times nothing more than a toss of the dice ... In essence, going off as a couple to do humanitarian work either has the couple intact at the end ... or not.

In a spirit of international development

International cooperation work is a delicate enterprise. It must be undertaken with the greatest of dexterity, with much humility and with constant apprenticeship in mind. Once on site, it is easy to become disillusioned. The problems encountered are at times so great that the efforts involved in our paltry offerings seem insignificant—even useless. Being realistic may be difficult but it is a must in order to survive the discouragement inherent in the ever present sea of poverty, corruption, injustice, human rights violations, and inequitable distribution of services and resources.

Over and above individual competencies must exist a personal aptitude that is more important than all others. Dr. Reine Lebel of Médecins Sans Frontières explains this in an interview: "Apart from a required resilience in order to accomplish anything in such work, an individual must have that sacred fire in the belly—that awareness of our own suffering. Before helping others, we must have healed ourselves, met our own needs. One of the most important things in such needy environments is 'presence.' We must take the time to establish connections, to listen, and with a calm and gentle voice to make known that we are there to meet the needs of the person encountered and not the needs we think that person needs. And because of this, presence is most crucial to the success of real humanitarian aid."

As relationships are the foundation of cooperative work, communication as well as patience are essential. Actually, social relationships are even more important than productivity or results. Quantifying results, therefore, must be reinterpreted. It is only through relationships that significant links and results can be achieved.

Professional Training

A priori, we cannot presume that Canadian experience in anything equates with valued experience in Africa or anywhere else.

International cooperation efforts are fruitful and satisfying for all concerned only in as much as workers are well prepared, well equipped and "available" to those in need. Success occurs only when a fruitful encounter "happens" for both the giver and the receiver.

Before taking flight into this unknown universe, time should be invested in order to assure a higher potential for success. The link between theory and practice should be reviewed in pre-departure training with on-site group experiences organized under the trained eye of experts.

If I had followed an in-depth course in international development, I would most probably have had a better understanding of the work I was setting out to do—and my experience would have been a more fulfilling one—both for me and for those I set out to assist.

It is important to understand the goals before taking on a quest.

Non-governmental organizations—post-experience support

Non-governmental organizations (NGOs) invest a lot to send their international development/ aid workers abroad. They cover travel, medical insurance and subsistence costs. Would it not be better if those same NGOs allotted a decent sum to assist those same workers to adapt and integrate more easily to the job as well as their return home? In light of the difficulties international development/ aid workers face in coming back home, would it not be sensible to greet and support those persons in their reintegration process? Should it be the sole responsibility of the international development/ aid worker to readapt on his or her own? Or is it a shared responsibility?

Take for example the Armed Forces, which have adopted a program for soldiers returning from missions and who suffer from operational stress injuries (OSI)—OSI being the most recent term used for PTSD. Throughout Canada, the military has established support units as well as an Internet site offering pertinent information and guidance.

Follow-ups of personnel returning from any stressful environment are a necessity, not a luxury. Employers are responsible for the well-being of persons they employ and should support them both in the field and upon their return. A psychiatrist trained in the field of international aid is the person who would be most capable of recognizing the danger signs of distress—and this at the most crucial stage of reintegration.

NGOs offer pre-assignment programs and various levels of support during assignments. These are important especially when new aid workers are on their first encounter with a different world.

Workers should know they can speak of their experiences to those who would understand. Letting off steam should be a norm rather than a possibility. But then recognized needs around the world are many. Every dollar spent in goods and services needs to be accounted for. How do we then justify the importance of investing in the well-being of the personnel? As well, there is always the problem of overwork for those in supervisory positions and the threat of lower funding through loss of governmental grants. This adds to administrative tensions.

Nonetheless, NGOs should be encouraged to have their own professional support programs for both on-site and returning personnel.

If our soldiers have lived through actual war scenarios and other negative experiences, international development/ aid workers may have also experienced wars of a different kind—those where lands and people have been ravaged by poverty, corruption, and injustice for years. The reality may not be overly aggressive, yet the damage done is nonetheless still real.

As stated previously, choosing to venture out into a world of international cooperation and humanitarian aid is laudable but demands serious preparation and a review of motives, of our capacity to survive stress-related situations and of our professional competencies.

Competency essentials
Profile of the Interculturally Effective Person[29]

Adaptation skills	Interculturally Effective Persons (IEPs) are those who have the ability to adapt personally and professionally to the conditions and challenges they encounter in the culture to which they are aspiring to offer humanitarian aid.
An attitude of modesty and respect	IEPs must both recognize the importance and the limitations of their offering to a culture into which they will be inserting themselves through an offer of counsel. A capacity to integrate, embrace and take into account established cultural frameworks is essential. Workers must display a willingness to adapt, to learn from the milieu—and this through consultation with those affected if due respect is to be felt by the recipients of aid.

---

[29] Summary from Vulpe, Thomas, Daniel Kealey, David Protheroe and Doug Macdonald, *A Profile of the Interculturally Effective Person*, Centre for Intercultural Learning, Department of Foreign Affairs and International Trade, 2000.

An understanding of the concept of culture	IEPs must comprehend the concept of culture and its omnipresent influence on the daily lives of those being assisted as well as the lives of those assisting.
Knowledge of the host country and culture	IEPs have more than a basic knowledge of the country and its culture if their work is to be in any way productive and positive.
Relationship building	IEPs must possess excellent interpersonal skills.
Self knowledge	IEPs must be self-aware—conscious of their own roots and motivations as well as their strengths and weaknesses.
Intercultural communication	To be most efficient in carrying out their on-site responsibilities, IEPs must be super-comfortable in the exercise of intercultural communications.
Organizational skills	IEPs must have, as a force, the recognition that their duties involve the improvement of non-existent or already established structures in the areas where aid is required. If team goals are to be realized there must be a recognition of the need to add or maintain a high level of morale in the already established or to be created team spirit.
Personal and professional commitment	Personal and professional involvement in "other than our own" cultural environments is essential to the positive outcome of any and all aid being proffered.

Post-Traumatic Stress Disorder Symptoms

Post-traumatic Stress Disorder (PTSD) is included in a new chapter in DSM-5 (Diagnostic and Statistical Manual of Mental Disorders). The American Psychiatric Association (APA) has published DSM-5 in 2013, culminating a 14-year revision process. This new edition of the manual is used by clinicians and researchers to diagnose and classify mental disorders.

Among several changes in the new DSM, PTSD moves from being addressed as an anxiety disorder to a Trauma- and Stressor-Related Disorder. The diagnostic criteria identify the trigger to PTSD as exposure to actual or threatened death, serious injury or sexual violation. The exposure must result from one or more of the following scenarios, in which the individual:

- directly experiences the traumatic event;
- witnesses the traumatic event in person;
- learns that the traumatic event occurred to a close family member or close friend (with the actual or threatened death being either violent or accidental); or
- experiences first-hand repeated or extreme exposure to aversive details of the traumatic event (not through media, pictures, television or movies unless work-related).

The disturbance, regardless of its trigger, causes clinically significant distress or impairment in the individual's social interactions, capacity to work and/or other important areas of functioning.

DSM-5 proposes four distinct diagnostic categories as opposed to three.

RE-EXPERIENCING:
- Flashbacks;
- Spontaneous memories of the traumatic event;
- Recurrent dreams related to the traumatic event;

- Other intense or prolonged psychological distress.

AVOIDANCE
- Distressing memories, thoughts, feelings or external reminders of the event(s)

NEGATIVE COGNITIONS AND MOOD
- Persistent and distorted sense of blame of self or others;
- Myriad of feelings;
- Estrangement from others;
- Markedly diminished interest in activities;
- Inability to remember key aspects of the event(s).

AROUSAL
- Aggressive, reckless or self-destructive behavior;
- Sleep disturbances;
- Hypervigilance or related problems.

References

BROWN, Brené, PhD, *Daring Greatly*, Penguin Group, New York, USA, 2012, 245 pp.

BROWN, Brené, PhD, *I Thought It Was Just Me*, Penguin Group, New York, USA, 2007, 303 pp.

DISPENZA, Dr. Joe, *Breaking the Habit of Being Yourself*, Hay House, Inc., Carlsbad, USA, 2012, 329 pp.

DYER, Dr. Wayne, *Inspiration*, Hay House, Inc., Carlsbad, USA, 2006, 255 pp.

FRANKL, Victor, *Man's Search for Meaning*, Beacon Press, Boston, USA, 2006, 165 pp.

GREENBERGER, Dennis, PhD and Christine A. PADESKY, PhD, *Mind Over Mood*, Second Edition, The Guilford Press, New York, USA, 1995, 215 pp.

HAY, Louise L., *You Can Heal Your Life*, Hay House, Inc., Carlsbad, USA, 2004, 253 pp.

HANH, Thich Nhat, *You Are Here*, Shambhala Publications Inc., Boston, USA, 2009, 143 pp.

HANSON, Rick, PhD and Richard MENDIUS, MD, *Buddha's Brain*, New Harbinger Publications, Inc., Oakland, USA, 2009, 272 pp.

HARRIS, Dan, *10% Happier: How I Tamed the Voice in My Head, Reduced Stress Without Losing My Edge and Found Self-Help That Actually Works—A True Story*, Dey Street Books, USA, 2014, 256 pp.

JOBIN, Anne-Marie, *Le Journal Créatif*, Éditions du Roseau, Montréal, Canada, 2002, 259 pp.

LAGACÉ, Jacqueline, PhD, *The End of Pain: How Nutrition and Diet Can Fight Chronic Inflammatory Disease*, Greystone Books Ltd., USA, 2014, 288 pp.

MARI, Jean-Paul, *Sans blessures apparentes*, Éditions Robert Laffont, Paris, France, 2008, 306 pp.

PALMER, Helen, *The Enneagram: Understanding Yourself and the Others in Your Life*, HarperCollins Publishers, New York, USA, 1991, 418 pp.

SINGER, Michael, *The Untethered Soul*, New Harbinger Publications Inc., Oakland, USA, 2007, 181 pp.

TOLLE, Eckhart, *Stillness Speaks*, Namaste Publishing, Vancouver, Canada, 2003, 129 pp.

TOLLE, Eckhart, *The Power of Now*, Namaste Publishing, Vancouver, Canada, 1999, 240 pp.

VULPE, Thomas, Daniel KEALEY, David PROTHEROE and Doug MACDONALD, *A Profile of the Interculturally Effective Person*, Centre for Intercultural Learning, Department of Foreign Affairs and International Trade, 2000, 62 pp.

Magazines

SOLAMA, Peter, *Humanitarian Exchange Magazine*, Issue 15, "Psychological Health of Relief Workers"

TICK, Edward, *Light of Consciousness*, Volume 23, "Return of the Ghost Dancers"

Internet sites

www.homecomingvets.wordpress.com

www.canineswithacause.org

www.OSISS.ca

www.mentalhealthrecovery.com/wrap-is/

Acknowledgements

My most heartfelt appreciation goes out to:

My husband, for his unconditional love and support.

My father, for his commitment to this writing project, the countless hours spent translating.

My step-daughter, Orlane, for her smile, her sensitivity, her joyous presence.

My family, for their encouragement and their support.

My friends, for their compassion and their comfort.

Lieutenant-General the Honourable Roméo Dallaire (Ret), for his precious counsel.

Benoît Cazabon, for his coaching, advice and generosity.

Philippe Nolet, for the many hours spent revising the initial manuscript.

Syd Gravel and his wife Judy, for their precious feedback.

Dan Bowers, for an inspiring book title.

Dr. Lina Charette, for her professionalism, respect and encouragement.

My guardian angel, **Catherine Doherty**.